Career Development

A 21st Century Job Search Handbook

Career Development

A 21st Century Job Search Handbook

Monica E. Breidenbach

PRENTICE HALL
Upper Saddle River, NJ 07458

Library of Congress Cataloging-in-Publication Data

Breidenbach, Monica E.
    Career development : a 21st-century job search handbook / Monica
E. Breidenbach. -- 3rd ed.
        p.   cm.
    Includes bibliographical references and index.
    ISBN 0-13-576588-9
    1. Career development.   I. Title.
HF5549.5.C35B74   1998
650.14--dc21   98-39572
                                                                 CIP

Acquisitions Editor: Todd Rossell
Production Editor: Dawn Sitzmann
Production Liaison: Eileen M. O'Sullivan
Managing Editor: Mary Carnis
Director of Manufacturing and Production: Bruce Johnson
Manufacturing Buyer: Marc Bove
Marketing Manager: Frank Mortimer, Jr.
Editorial Assistant: Amy Diehl
Formatting/page make-up: Carlisle Publishers Services
Printer/Binder: Banta Harrisonburg
Cover Design: Pat Wosczyk

 ©1998 by Prentice-Hall, Inc.
Simon & Schuster/A Viacom Company
Upper Saddle River, New Jersey 07458

Printed in the United States of America

10   9   8   7   6   5   4   3   2   1

ISBN 0-13-576588-9

Prentice-Hall International (UK) Limited, *London*
Prentice-Hall of Australia Pty. Limited, *Sydney*
Prentice-Hall Canada Inc., *Toronto*
Prentice-Hall Hispanoamericana, S.A., *Mexico*
Prentice-Hall of India Private Limited, *New Delhi*
Prentice-Hall of Japan, Inc., *Tokyo*
Simon & Schuster Asia Pte. Ltd., *Singapore*
Editora Prentice-Hall do Brasil, Ltda., *Rio de Janeiro*

This work is lovingly dedicated to Verda Hunter, M.D., oncologist/gynecologist, who saved my life, Kathleen Koeltzow, clinical nurse specialist, who guided me through chemotherapy, and Mary O'Halloran, who assisted and nursed me back to health. Their care supported me and enabled me to complete this work. I am most grateful for their advocacy and continued support.

Contents

Foreword

Cutting-edge technology meets the graduating candidates for jobs now and in the 21st century. Technology and job searchers need to meet and make a pact with each other. Candidates for new jobs, graduating from our universities, and the advancing explosive developments in technology could form a partnership that is unbeatable. Using technology to locate the best jobs for the best candidates will propel the newest professionals in the marketplace to the frontline positions.

You may question why one uses technology to do a job search. The reasons are quite clear:

1. You are a candidate for a challenging position.
2. You live in a new age where technology explodes with new options daily.
3. User-friendly software abounds.
4. Amazing hardware exists to assist you to locate the best job for yourself.

First, technology is one of the least-expensive ways to gain the widest access to opportunities. It is a forum for many decision makers to see and measure new graduates' capabilities, education, experience, availability, and readiness for particular jobs in certain industries.

Second, technology is now multitasked to assist the searcher to locate positions and businesses of interest easily and to find business profiles that clearly depict what a company does, who runs the company, and the company's annual revenue.

Third, technology can show you your competitors' résumés so that you can understand who is out there looking for the same jobs you are. You can identify credentials needed to compete with them for the jobs available.

Fourth, you can survey the salary guides and compare what is appropriate for your type of experience, education, and interest in a particular field or position. All you need to know is how to use a modem. Most public libraries have an Internet connection, but it is usually not interactive. You can do your research and print the data you need or want, but you cannot send anything in response unless you have your own access code or e-mail address.

However, this text is not just an electronic job search manual. I suggest that you use all three methods to search for the best possible job:

- Traditional process (e.g., ads, graduate-placement offices, agencies, applications, résumé, letters, calendar, and interviews)
- Network techniques (expand the list of who you know)
- Electronics technology (multitasked, easy, inexpensive, broad-based, and focused)

The traditional process will be the easiest for some because it is familiar to them or their advisers. Most books are about this long-recognized approach. Most traditional managers will be comfortable with this routine approach and easily recognize what you are doing as a candidate. The tools of cover letters, résumés, and interviews are very familiar to them. But all managers are not in this category, and all businesses are not limited to this recognized kind of search method.

Networking is a contemporary tool to build access to leaders and decision makers in a chosen field or industry. This also is familiar to most managers and decision makers who understand all the tools and processes a well-qualified candidate must use to find the best possible job. These leaders also use this same method when they are looking for talented employees to join their businesses. An executive's job is to find the best talent available in the market at a given time. Sometimes this takes place when decision makers meet the searchers who have penetrated the hidden market. These leaders can also be reached on the Internet.

Electronic job searching is the latest technique for gaining employment. It is the rocket that will send talented candidates into orbits of searching that are meant for them. The Internet, various software programs, and hardware equipment are the most used tools in an electronic search. The new talent is looking for jobs, and jobs are looking for new talent. They both speak the same language, use the same tools, respect the same expertise, and want to make the connection for the benefit of both.

This book directs one to use all three methods much as one would use a three-legged stool. All three legs are necessary for the stool to be useful. All three search methods need to be incorporated into a searcher's campaign in today's market because the market pool is so large, the competition is so aggressive, and the need is universal. Jobs are found in all three categories. Why not use all three options to maximize the opportunities?

Do not fall asleep in the cockpit of the new world rocket for technological job searching. You will miss your opportunity in the contemporary job market.

Preface

Welcome to the opportunity of a lifetime. With this book you have a ticket to a contemporary launch site where career searchers begin to look for options that are near and far. Why do you have such an advantage? The book presumes job searchers are aware of how the digital age can help them conduct a job search.

Here are the tools to help you market your own education, experience, skills, and talents. You have the opportunity to market yourself twenty-four hours a day. Your visibility will be limited only by your access to the Internet, contemporary software packages that are available to help you, and your own imagination. This text has a programmed disk associated with it that will enable you to save important data and to bring your tools up to date quickly.

Access to the Internet will enable you to make your résumés available to the broadest possible audience in your chosen field. This text offers a three-tier career search that uses additional methods, human interaction, and modern technology. You will learn how to use all three to advantage.

Job security depends on your ability to use and improve technological search skills. Job searching is a matter of continuing education and lifelong attention to your career, the developments in your field, your own personal interests, and your needs to have a rewarding career with satisfying work.

You will not get today's or tomorrow's jobs with yesterday's techniques.

What Is in This Book?

Methodology, process, and techniques for a contemporary job search aimed primarily at recent college graduates are the focus of this text. The object is to present a three-pronged approach that will serve graduates in the contemporary marketplace, which is heavily saturated with skilled, educated, and experienced people willing to work for lower wages than their previous jobs afforded them.

This text is about organizing your life so that you will enjoy a great search and uncover various opportunities to consider for future job possibilities. This text uses all three aspects of job searching. The time-honored techniques identified are the traditional, the contemporary techniques known as networking, and the new challenges of technology and software that will give wings to your search and make you visible everywhere twenty-four hours a day.

What Is Not in This Book?

This text is not focused on one method over another. All three methods of job searching work. Each of the three methods is more respected in and applicable to different fields. This text does not give examples to copy but rather identifies the philosophy behind why one procedure is better than another; for instance, why is it important to tell a potential interviewer that you will call him or her to arrange a meeting rather than waiting to be called after sending your letter and request for an interview?

This book does not teach you how to use technology or specific hardware or software. It presumes that you are willing to learn the details from a more knowledgeable source than a book on job searching. The tools are available. When to use the tools is the main purpose of the directives suggested in this book.

How Is This Book Organized?

This book is organized the way one would go about an actual search regarding time, depth of research, development of tools to conduct a search, methods for keeping track of appointments, evaluating interviews, classifying information gathered, and targeting the appropriate use of one's time, money, energy, and other resources to complete a successful search.

Who Should Use This Book?

Recent graduates of degree programs who want to change their current positions or improve their current professional condition but stay with their current employers will find helpful information. The text will assist individuals with newly acquired degrees or certifications to use their education in the workplace. Counselors and advisers of graduates can use this text to maximize the market for their protégés. Professional associations and alumnae/alumni associations, which have workshops or seminars to assist their members to find better positions than they currently hold, might adapt this text material to seminars and workshops.

Acknowledgments

No book of this dimension is the work of one person. There are many people whose work and support I wish to acknowledge, including students and professional clients who have continued over the years to express their ideas, react to my suggestions, challenge the validity of my strategies, and completed many and varied satisfied career searches. In addition, I appreciate the work of students who tested and retested the design of the *Career Planner* in appendix I over two years of research, building, testing, rebuilding, and so forth.

Special thanks to all those friends who understood when I needed time to work on this task. Chief among them are Jan Lowery and Lea Endlich. Chris Adams, the Prentice-Hall representative for our school, deserves special mention; her support with retaining my efforts at Prentice-Hall has been spectacular. We have traveled together down a long road with this task.

Professional educators who have commented, evaluated, and measured these concepts; taught and tested these ideas in the classroom; and contributed their own suggestions to this book's continuing development are Dr. Maris Roze, DeVRY Inc., Oak Terrace, Illinois; Dean Simon Maxwell, Dr. Pat Decker, Professors Cindy Newburg, Jan Norman, and Martin Ward, and the Computer Lab Supervisor John Fuhrman, DeVRY Institute of Technology, Kansas City; Provost James Billick, Dr. Neal Harris, and Dr. Michael Sanchez, Ottawa University, Kansas City; Nancy Sheffler, speaker and coordinator of career day, Celesia Snyder, The Ohio State University; Rita Delude, New Hampshire and Community/Technical College; and others to whom I am grateful.

Last, but by no means least, are Dawn Sitzmann and her crew at Carlisle Publishers Services, Eileen O'Sullivan and Todd Rossell of Prentice Hall for their invaluable support and friendly guidance of this project to its completion.

Text Conversions

Text conversions are used as highlights throughout the text. These text conversions are labeled note, sidebar, think, tip, warning, employer focus, and searcher focus. This is information that the searcher may profit from reading. These ideas are not a part of the regular text but incidental to the context. They are offered throughout the text and are identified with the appropriate icons as illustrated below.

Note icon *indicates that additional information is available outside the regular text content.*

Warning icon *signifies that there is some problem looming on the horizon that may need the searcher's attention.*

Sidebar icon *indicates that additional information is available through interviewing or by doing more research.*

Employer focus icon *indicates a view decision makers might have about a searcher's ideas, presentation, questions, attitude, manners, and so forth.*

Think icon *indicates that there is a philosophical point or a general rule that applies to the directives given (there is no need to reinvent the wheel).*

Searcher focus icon *indicates suggestions referring to the searcher's mannerisms, enthusiasm, attitude, professionalism, and uniqueness.*

Tip icon *indicates an idea or suggestion that the searcher might consider using in his or her campaign.*

About the Author ...

■ **Dr. Monica E. Breidenbach**

Dr. Breidenbach has an enthusiasm for career management. She has been in the field since 1978 and has written two prior editions of the text. Her interest, knowledge, and experience is illustrated by the fact that each edition of this text has been rewritten to fit the market of the time. This one is no exception.

She is also a presenter of her ideas to national, regional, and local audiences. Her attitude is one of a "coach in your corner" while she assists collegians with their job pursuits upon completion of a degree award. Most of her time is spent teaching in colleges where career development and active graduate placement is the norm.

Her private practice includes working with people from all walks of life, ages 20-80, men and women, degreed and non-degreed, clerics, military, government, and corporate employees. She has also developed workshops for outplacement needs of companies. Her office can be reached through e-mail: *bbach7@hotmail.com,* if you have a career dilemma for which you want some direction, support, or advice.

Dr. Breidenbach is also a composer and a gardener. She loves to read, enjoys movies, theater, and concerts in her spare time, which she calls her renewing time. Monica has recently become successful in using a variety of computer application programs and some dBase programming. She designed and developed the *Career Planner,* which is available to students using the text, to keep track of all the data necessary to a professional search.

About the Book . . .

The new emphasis for this text:

1) Intense Focus on Marketing—Theory and Practice:
   - Skills Profile, Education, Experience
   - 24 hours a day, 7 days a week visibility
   - Business Profiles from Internet, Web sites, Infotrac

2) Technology use:
   - *Career Planner* DataBase Disk
   - Variety of Technical Résumé Formats
   - "Résumé float" for Internet Use

3) Covers 100 percent of the Market:
   - Traditional Professional Approach
   - Networking the Market of Choice
   - Multi-tasked Technology Potential

Career Development

A 21st Century Job Search Handbook

Segment 1

RESEARCH TECHNIQUES

■ *INTRODUCTION*

Now that you have completed all the papers you ever hope to write and have researched topic after topic for your various completed classes, it is important to begin using those same research skills in pursuit of the best job you can find in your field. There is a wide variety of resources available to you, including traditional libraries where those who may not have had access to the Internet could get an introduction. Often these libraries have career centers as a special service within the library itself. The print media are also available in well-managed and well-funded libraries of schools and communities.

Gathering leads and information about where the jobs are is another rich resource that career searchers may tap. Develop a journal and rely on your own abilities to research and find the right sources for you. Understand who you are and what you bring to this field of choice by way of your education, skill bases, and experience. In addition, do informational interviewing carefully because these conversations are some of the richest resources you have to mine.

Technology, wherever and however available, is invaluable in the present age. This includes the Internet, contemporary software packages, your own Web page, a video if needed, program disks, and a traditional résumé. Use as much of the developing technology as you understand and can reach.

These three ways of finding the right position for you are all tried and true. There is a résumé design and delivery method appropriate for every searcher and skill base.

The résumé often says more about YOU than it says about you!

Sound like double talk? Consider this: If you identify WordPerfect 6.0 as one of your skills or as a tool you know how to use, but your columns, margins, and so forth on the résumé are not perfectly aligned, the résumé says you don't know how to use this software even though you have stated you do. If you misspell words or use incorrect grammar you say volumes about your lack of

1

preparation for the business world. This will attract the eye of the reader immediately, no matter how good your résumé looks or how many degrees you have earned. Again, *the résumé says more about YOU, than it says about you!*

Chapters 1, 2, and 3 cover these matters in succession. Chapter 1 identifies resource centers for you to consider. Chapter 2 provides information about networking as a tool for research and information. Chapter 3 introduces challenges you need to consider. Join the cyberspace age and learn what is available for your use. Take advantage of all three approaches to the market. Then you will find the best job for you.

You are not looking for just any job. You are looking for the best job that matches your combination of education, skill base, and experience.

Chapter 1

LIBRARY RESOURCES

LEARNING OBJECTIVES

After you study this chapter, you should be able to

- Use a library's career center to your advantage.
- Delineate the various types of technology that are available to assist you with developing a solid research program to support your job search.
- Summarize the various print media titles that you know will be helpful to you and your research.
- Learn how to use InfoTrac or ProQuest to assist you with business profiles and business information.

- Develop some skill with the Internet and World Wide Web (WWW) for access to companies and their business profiles.
- Salary guides are available and updated daily in some instances. Become skillful enough to help yourself with this Internet tool.
- Discuss approaches to the hidden market with your colleagues to get peer advice and share what you have uncovered.

JOB SEARCH ISSUES / 21ST CENTURY _____

LIBRARY CAREER CENTER

InfoTrac
ProQuest

PRINT MEDIA

Newspapers
Directories
Journals
Financial Reports
Chambers of Commerce Literature

ELECTRONIC MEDIA

Software to Rent
Videotapes

Internet
CD-ROM
WWW

MARKET POTENTIAL

Open/Listed Markets
Hidden/Unlisted Markets

SKILLS

Internet
Basic Research
Technical
Software/Hardware

◼ *CAREER CENTERS*

Libraries are full of information and therefore are good sources for you to begin your job search. Libraries often have career centers where they have collected the materials about how to search for a job, as well as some of the business directories that are available to give you information about companies and industries. Libraries subscribe to newspapers and magazines. Several are available in hard copy, while others are on microfiche from which the information that is of interest to you can be printed.

InfoTrac is a subscription service for libraries that comes with a magazine-entries CD-ROM and a business-portfolio CD-ROM. Some libraries have a video screening room where you can view yourself to critique how you look and speak in an interview situation. Other libraries have information videos about the job searching process in one phase or another. The goal is to use as many resources as are available so that you will uncover as many jobs in your search as appeal to you.

Choosing one out of one is no choice.

Using the career center to your advantage often is as simple as telling the librarian what you are researching and asking for assistance in finding it. The more articulate you are about what you are investigating, the more the librarian can help you. Librarians are people who know where information is located and how to access it in a form useful to you—so ask!

◼ *PRINT MEDIA*

You say, "I don't know what it is I want to do 'when I grow up.'" Then you need to explore some possibilities in the field of your major or minor. You have educated yourself in a certain field. Begin

A word here about being focused. No one can help an unfocused person locate what even that individual cannot describe. Librarians are very talented and smart, but they cannot read your mind or intuit what might help you focus. So know what information you want before you approach them. This way you will get the best help in the fastest manner. Both you and the librarians will be happy.

there to look for companies that do what you want to do as a complete focus of their business or a subdivision of their overall business activity. Look up these companies by the SIC codes in the directories and with the variety of tools accessible in libraries.

You need to write letters of inquiry to companies you have discovered are in the business where you want to begin your career. You might also find, by using the SIC codes, that some businesses do what you want to do but only in one division. These businesses and companies can provide you with financial reports that will tell you much about the company. Remember, this information is from the company's viewpoint. You need to know what they think they are doing.

SIC codes are set by the U.S. Department of Labor, and their numbering system is explained in the beginning of most directories. The Dun & Bradstreet volumes have a clear explanation. The codes are consistent in all directories.

Next, write to your chosen companies and tell them why you are interested in them, how you came to know about them, and that you would like to receive copies of their latest financial reports, 10K reports (if they have one), and descriptive brochures about the specific interest you have, as well as a list of company establishments in the places you are planning to live. Some companies make a toll-free telephone number available to the public. Phone calls often provide quicker responses than letters, or you can contact companies on the Internet.

Other organizations you need to research are the various chamber of commerce offices where you are planning to live. If you have made up your mind already, it would not hurt to look at what the chamber of commerce has to say about the city it represents and what businesses are listed as members of the chamber. In your letter of inquiry to the chambers of commerce, list the things you want in a city. Chambers often make toll-free numbers available also.

Good manners are always appreciated in business settings. They reveal an individual who is courteous, educated, sensitive, knowledgeable, and professional about how to request information.

Think about where you have lived and where you are living now. What appeals to you about these cities? Remember that chambers of commerce can give you information about things to do outside of the workplace. They provide information about weather, taxes, newspapers, city services, travel, sports, arts, movies, crime statistics, and accessibility of grocery stores, drug stores, and medical facilities. What do you want to know about the city? What city services would you need or want to have available?

■ *ELECTRONIC MEDIA*

The library CD-ROM InfoTrac and ProQuest collections of magazine articles and microfiche copies of newspapers and journal articles can be researched for recent information about companies and cities of interest. If something good or not-so-good has happened in a city or occurred in a company, chances are that someone in the last six months has written about it to analyze it, research it, and compare it to other like companies, cities, and industries. These current sources of information are invaluable to you when considering a company as a potential employer or a city as your next home.

Many college libraries have purchased ProQuest, which is a CD-ROM that will access periodicals under headings of "Business Journals" and "General Reading Periodicals." This enables you to read the article on screen, but it can also be printed if you want to have a hard copy of the article. The topics of interest can be searched by keyword, topic, or periodical—if known. Like InfoTrac, this is a rich resource for information about companies, businesses, and cities of interest to the searcher.

This chapter has delineated the help available in the modern college library and city libraries. Information may be available through a career center if one is established within a library. You can maximize your use of the information available through the business directories, print media, and technology most commonly found in today's library. These sources have been updated in focus, dimension, and use of technology. They are the traditional resources available to searchers.

Chapter 1 Challenges

Technology

1. Get to know your local librarian and ask for assistance in using InfoTrac, ProQuest, the Internet, and any other access software that the library can provide for your research. Record on a calendar whether you have been clear enough with the librarian to get the precise information you need.
2. Graph the print media, electronic media, and personal interviewing contributions to your research, your information base, and your support.
3. Repeat the second challenge, but this time graph the usefulness of hardware, software, Internet access, and the WWW.
4. Illustrate with a time line or chart how you can be in the market twenty-four hours a day, seven days a week.
5. Identify the traditional forces described in chapter 1 and graph how this method could help you achieve your career goal.

Traditional

1. Describe your approach to the "hidden market."
2. Outline all the search tools you intend to use and what each tool can help you achieve for research and strategy.
3. Analyze the usefulness of technology in your individual search process. What do you expect it to do for you?
4. What does it mean to be a professional in your chosen field?
5. List the technological ways one can use to present résumé information.
6. What does the following sentence mean? "Choosing one out of one is no choice."
7. How can the print media help you with your search?

Vocabulary

Formulate at least sixteen of the following words into a crossword puzzle with rows and columns. Exchange with classmates. Supply answer sheet as instructor designates.

agencies	financial report	print media
business portfolio	information interviews	ProQuest
business directories	InfoTrac	résumé
career centers	Internet	SIC codes
CD-ROM	journal	Web
chambers of commerce	microfiche	10K report
cyberspace age		

Chapter 2

PERSONAL RESOURCES

LEARNING OBJECTIVES

After studying this chapter you should be able to

- Explain how to use the richness of friends and business associates to help you locate the best possible job.
- Differentiate between your skills and personal characteristics.
- Describe who you are in relation to work.
- Compare and contrast your skills.
- Analyze your accomplishments for your natural skills and characteristics.
- Keep a personal journal.

- Build a support group.
- Prepare to do informational interviewing.
- Use the Internet for electronic networking.
- Send your résumé into cyberspace.
- Use the dBase disk to keep track of your progress.
- Prepare a position-wanted ad for your local newspaper.
- Prepare two lists of companies: one you will use for informational interviewing and the other for job interviews.

LEARNING PROCESSES / SKILLS

PERSONAL RESOURCES

Relatives
Friends
Business Associates
College Groups
Teachers, Coaches, Mentors
Managers
Business Peers/Customers
Salespeople

ELECTRONIC MARKETING

Internet
Networking

CYBERSPACE CONNECTIONS

Managers/Directors
Computer "Nerds"
Internet

SKILLS

Software
Personal Analysis
Hardware
Decision Making
Self Knowledge
Writing
Interpersonal
dBase
Interviewing
Introspection
Communication

■ *PERSONAL DATA GATHERING*

Individuals bring their individuality, creativity, imagination, stamina, and energy to a search. These personal resources will be used again and again as a unit and separately as the search campaign continues its course. It is important that individuals know and understand what has gone on before the search began in order to better understand the qualities they have to support themselves and the characteristics they want a potential employer to know they possess.

Knowing who you are is your secret weapon. The goal is to begin understanding what you bring to the marketplace with your accumulated education, experience, skills, and characteristics. Your goal is not to become someone else you admire. After you have completed the personal database, you will be able to think about what you have as strengths and weaknesses and what you want to become as a professional, with the challenges and obstacles that field represents. Your self-esteem must be high and you must know everything about yourself.

What do you have to offer? How do you know this is true about you? Where are the resources you have used to get this far in your pursuit of a career? Analyze yourself on the next page and take a good look at who is stepping into the professional marketplace. Think about your answers. This is your life!

PERSONAL INFORMATION

List the characteristics, traits, virtues, strengths, skills, and talents that have revealed themselves in your life in the following three categories. Use the information from appendix F, as well as considering

Family (including family of generation, of origin, hobbies, economics, stress, success, and so on):

Employment (including all your jobs, military service, volunteer activities):

Education (including all levels of schooling situations):

_____   _____   _____

_____   _____   _____

_____   _____   _____

_____   _____   _____

_____   _____   _____

_____   _____   _____

_____   _____   _____

_____   _____   _____

_____   _____   _____

_____   _____   _____

_____   _____   _____

_____   _____   _____

_____   _____   _____

_____   _____   _____

_____   _____   _____

_____   _____   _____

_____   _____   _____

_____   _____   _____

■ *PROFESSIONAL AND PERSONAL ACCOMPLISHMENTS*

Looking back over your life there are many accomplishments to evaluate. Identify accomplishments that you feel are most significant to you. These can be professional, personal, educational, or family-related experiences.

To evaluate your past and present in light of your future potential, it is necessary to determine the skills you have and the personality characteristics you possess that are illustrated throughout your chosen accomplishments in one way or another. Achievements occur in relationship to situations or conditions that are initiated or improved as a result of your ideas and efforts.

In business or professional accomplishments, indicate improvement in terms of benefit to the organization—you helped it make money, save money, use talent creatively, improve efficiency, identify problem areas, and reduce waste, to name a few. In personal accomplishments, list characteristics and projects that brought you personal satisfaction.

Write out five accomplishments in the following outline:

The situation was . . .
I did . . .
The results were . . .

ACCOMPLISHMENT #1 _____

The situation in which I found myself was

Analysis Column

I decided to

The results were

ACCOMPLISHMENT #2

The situation in which I found myself was

Analysis Column

I decided to

The results were

ACCOMPLISHMENT #3 _____

The situation in which I found myself was

Analysis Column

I decided to

The results were

ACCOMPLISHMENT #4 _____

The situation in which I found myself was

Analysis Column

I decided to

The results were

ACCOMPLISHMENT #5 _____

The situation in which I found myself was   Analysis Column

I decided to

The results were

From the analysis column in each of these five accomplishments, transfer the skills and characteristics to page 11 under the appropriate heading.

Research any evaluations you may have from peers, professors, clients, customers, and former and present managers. Read these evaluations and select the words that describe your attitudes as a worker and your skills in the department. Add these to the list on page 11.

SKILLS / CHARACTERISTICS ANALYSIS AND PRIORITIES

The criteria for skills identity and priority are

1. You like doing this
2. You are good at doing this
3. You want to use this skill in your
   next job

The criteria for characteristics identity are

1. You are pleased with this characteristic
2. You like people to know this about you
3. You want to be able to use this characteristic
   in your next job

Look at the list on page 11. Separate the skills from the characteristics; separate things you can do from the way you are. If a skill or characteristic meets the three criteria listed, it can make it to your top-ten list. It does not matter if you do not fill the columns.

Top Skills

_____

_____

_____

_____

_____

_____

_____

_____

_____

_____

Top Characteristics

_____

_____

_____

_____

_____

_____

_____

_____

_____

_____

Fantasy Goal Statement

Look at these top skills and characteristics and select the best three in each column and develop a fantasy goal statement. Imagine what kind of a job would require these three skills and characteristics. Write that job description here. Do not be concerned about whether you have ever heard of such a job. The important focus is for you to describe a job that best makes use of the skills and characteristics you want to use.

_____

_____

_____

_____

_____

_____

Real-Life Career Position Wanted

Using the same skills and characteristics, develop a brief recap of your current job readiness (thirty-five to fifty words) that would describe you and your dreams. Give yourself a job title and briefly describe yourself in terms of these three skills and characteristics. If you have never seen a position-wanted ad you may want to look at one in the classified section of your local newspaper. Some candidates put their position-wanted ads in *The Wall Street Journal.* To start, you may want to place yours in the local newspaper to see what happens.

_____

_____

_____

_____

_____

■ *PERSONAL JOURNAL*

Another useful tool is to keep a journal of your activities during a job search campaign. This is a consistent way to watch yourself grow and change given the experiences you are having. We grow and change constantly, but most of us do not take the time to write down how incidents, arguments, friendships, books, movies, TV shows, and so forth affect us.

At the end of each day or week summarize key learning, happenings, experiences, and challenges that occurred to you in that time frame. This can be an interview, a movie, a conversation with a friend, a class session, or a chance meeting. The incident does not matter; what matters is that you want to remember it for some reason. These things belong in your journal. Your journal is private and for no one else to see unless you give permission.

Start your journal entry with one of the following phrases. This will keep your journal from becoming trite and seeming useless to you as a revelation tool for your growth and development. You will grow tremendously during a career search campaign. If you do not already keep track of the major things that happen in your life, this is a good place to start.

Journal entries:

> It is now clear to me that . . .
> Questions I still have . . .
> Concerns that are worrying me . . .
> As a result of this meeting, or class, I will . . .
> At our next meeting I want to remember to . . .
> When I see this person again I will be happier if . . .
> Follow-up I need to do includes . . .
> Looking at my life today I now realize that . . .

▪ *BUILDING A SUPPORT GROUP*

Building a support group is no easier or more difficult than building a group of friends. Know how much time and advice you want from each member of your support group. This way you can negotiate for the time you need and keep people in the inner circle that advises you during this campaign. Who is available for this task depends on the situations people are in at the moment.
Some sources to consider (you only need four to six people):

Counselor   _____

Professor   _____

Relative   _____

Spouse   _____

Business Associate   _____

Classmate   _____

Good Friend   _____

Person in the Field   _____

Others   _____

   Tell people exactly what you want from them in terms of level of advice, knowledge of job searching, knowledge of your professional field, time, and method of meeting with them. There is no reason why all must meet at once unless you need that; remember that it will be very difficult to schedule such a meeting. Graciously accept whatever people say they can give you. These people will be the most helpful group you will have during this search process if they are clear about what you want from them.

▪ *INFORMATIONAL INTERVIEWING*

The next group that will be helpful to you in your campaign is individuals, from whatever source, who agree to speak with you about the industry, your capabilities of entering the industry, and their

Informational interviewing appears to many young people to be a waste of time because all they want to do is interview for the jobs. This method is how you will uncover the best possible position for you. You can interview the day after graduation, be offered a job, and accept the job without knowing your own potential in the marketplace.

judgment about the future of the industry. They are a rich source of leads to other people you should know and meet.

Networking is the perfect tool for identifying which decision makers are looking for you. Often we do not use networking effectively, and it is the one tool that can and should be used every waking hour. "You network with your feet," according to one humorist, meaning that you should be networking when you are walking your dog, plowing through the grocery aisles, shopping in a mall, standing in line for a movie, sitting next to someone on a bus, meeting people at parties, anywhere, anytime. Anyone who does not know you or your goals to find a great position should hear from you about your objectives.

This is a most productive tool because people are hidden away from their professional markets while they are employed. "No need to be looking," they say. Or while they are going to school. "No time to look," they say. It is the best place and time to get the most current information from the day-to-day workers in your career field. These people know what is happening and often are willing to share what they know with you. Take advantage of their wisdom. Talk with them.

Use your personal skills and characteristics to advantage. Understand yourself to the maximum. Analyze your gifts and skills efficiently. Develop a journalistic style to keep track of your success. Ask for support from people who know you and want you to succeed. This is how to get time with decision makers. Do not put any naysayers in your group. You do not need that while you are searching for a job; the campaign is hard enough. What you need are realistic feedback, informed analysis, genuine interest in your success, pertinent information about the field, and personal support.

Use the network route to explore the field, the options, and the businesses, and to see what is out there. Next explore by comparing one company to another. Which is best for you? Where will you get the kind of good start everyone needs when beginning a venture like a new career? Network everywhere, in all kinds of places, with everyone you meet. Your job search is no secret. The more people you know, the more people there are to assist you. Informational interviewing is used by professionals all the time. If you are going to join their ranks, then proceed as they do, enlisting others to assist you in getting where you want to go.

There is no place or time to be shy. Self-effacement is really not a virtue, but a subterfuge, and basically unworthy of a successful searcher.

■ *ELECTRONIC NETWORKING*

Take time to network well. The information interview is an old technique that comes alive on the Internet. It is not synonymous with "sneaky" job interviewing, as some searchers feel. Originally the purpose of informational interviewing was the secret element for job searchers to see decision makers who might have jobs. More importantly, they were sought for their advice and counsel. If a searcher landed at the right time and in the right places a job could be offered.

This is what has been called breaking into the "hidden market." The hidden market is the unlisted market. It consists of jobs that are going to be open but are not yet listed. It also includes new jobs that are about to be created. Take advantage of technology and do your informational interviewing over the Internet. You can use gopher and Telnet. Gopher access is free, so the price is right.

gopher://DARTCMS1.DARTMOUTH.EDU:70/11/FEDJOBS

Newsnet is a sophisticated electronic news-clipping service you can search by topic. Get information by calling the Newsnet help desk (**800-395-1301**).

Why would someone talk with you on the 'Net? On computers people seem to be more likely to answer questions, share information, make referrals, and even invite you to meet them somewhere for an interview. This cyberspace connection has a tendency to make both parties more relaxed, since there is less pressure to perform. Computer interaction is often considered a hobby by highly placed executives and managers. Additionally, they are communicating with you on their personal time rather than company time.

Chapter 2 has capitalized on using the personal side of one's growth and development to advantage while job searching. It advises searchers to incorporate enabling others to assist them in achieving their goals. The support group and network contacts help by participating with searchers to complete their campaign.

Chapter 2 Challenges

Technology

1. Use the disk in appendix I to keep track of your data.
2. Illustrate who you think you are in some graphical format. Give your illustration to someone you know and see if they recognize you.
3. Chart your accomplishments by identifying and organizing your skills and characteristics given the value you feel they deserve in relation to your life so far.
4. Write a position-wanted ad and put it in your daily paper. Track the responses for two weeks and chart the results.
5. Use a chart to evaluate the contribution you hope each member of your support group will make. Evaluate again after your first serious nibble, after three weeks of your campaign, and at the end of your campaign. Compare these three charts at the end of your search. What have you learned about people?

Traditional

1. Identify some businesses and industries where you think your fantasy goal statement would make sense and profit. Why do you think so?

2. Design and keep a personal journal from research to job acceptance throughout your entire marketing campaign.
3. What do you expect to come from informational interviewing?
4. Explain your understanding of the networking process and how it will help your campaign.
5. Why should electronic networking be advantageous to you? to the other person?

Vocabulary

Develop an expository essay that would use at least twenty-five of the following words to explain why personal contacts are a rich source of information in a *career search* process.

accomplishment	hidden market	personality
achievement	hobbies	position-wanted ad
campaign	informational interviews	priorities
candidate	job description	professional
characteristics	job interviews	self-esteem
contacts	job search	skills
decision makers	leads	strengths
economics	markets	support group
electronic networking	naysayers	talent
evaluations	negotiate	Telnet
goal statement	'Net	traits
gopher	Newsnet	virtues
		volunteer

Chapter 3

TECHNOLOGY AND THE JOB SEARCH

LEARNING OBJECTIVES

After studying this chapter, you should be able to

- Define technology in light of its potential usefulness in a job search.
- List the kinds of hardware you know how to use and adapt to a job search.
- Graph the many different kinds of software you have mastered and determine how these software packages could be helpful in your job search.
- Illustrate what a multimedia résumé would look like if you have already acquired the skills.

- What would your multimedia résumé say about you to the potential viewer of your résumé?
- Explain how the Internet could be helpful in a career search.
- Customize your résumé to fit you and you alone.
- Prepare a résumé for floating on the Internet. Convert your data to ASCII text to do this. Add keyword stripe.
- Develop a slide presentation for the information you want on your résumé.

LEARNING PROCESSES / SKILLS

TECHNOLOGY

Hardware/Software

SOFTWARE SYSTEMS

Applications
Operating Systems
Languages
Programming
Networks

RÉSUMÉS

Customized
ASCII Text
PowerPoint Slide Show
Demo Disks

INTERNET

Multimedia
Web Site
Research
Interactive Disk

OTHER MEDIA

Videotape
FAX
Database

HARDWARE

Computers
Printers
Peripherals

Technology has given lightning speed and twenty-four-hour access to potential employers. Individuals with good technical skills will find using this method, as well as the previous two discussed in chapters 1 and 2 , an inexpensive and very contemporary method for job searching. This chapter is about technology that is helpful to individuals in finding the best possible job available.

■ *HARDWARE*

There are hardware and software issues to understand and use effectively beyond those already described in chapter 1. Access to the Internet and the tremendous boon that it is to make employers aware of technically talented people looking for jobs is the newest access for employers and an often neglected tool of job hunters. Using a video presentation is another way to "go for an interview" when it is impossible for you to be there in person.

Let us begin with hardware. The simplest need for hardware is a laser printer that gives you a crisp, brilliant image with the blackest ink on white paper. In America there is no substitute for a

You may want to use colored stationery. Buy a ream of paper. At the same time, buy 250 matching envelopes. Take 100 sheets of the paper to the printer for your résumé. Use the rest for letters you will need to write. You will not overbuy this way. The only acceptable colors are ivory, pewter, and beige. Absolutely no shades of pastels may be used. Only use the blackest ink, no matter the color of paper.

clean, clear, concise, one-page, focused résumé. If you do not have access to such hardware yourself there are commercial establishments that will print your résumés for you. Bring your own paper. It costs less and you will be able to match colors better. Sometimes even white can be different shades.

The clearest résumés can be created with a variety of hardware if the user knows how to use the equipment and the software in tandem. Poorly produced résumés are the result of the operator, not the equipment.

The clue here is to use what you know how to use effectively. Buy the services of others for that which you cannot do successfully. You just may not have enough experience with the process and/or the equipment.

■ *SOFTWARE*

Software is amazing in its variety and complexity. And yet it becomes easy for some because they understand the software and have worked with it until they truly understand it. You can find software that will write your résumé for you, but templates are rigid. There is a software program that accompanies this text (see appendix I). Read the directions and follow them. Some of these data will lead to a creative résumé that you like because you compose it. This disk is a great way to gather and keep all the research data you have collected and will need and use in your campaign. This is not a résumé-making tool but a database system for your use. Good luck!

You can buy expensive software that will do everything and anything. Shop carefully. You may not need all the bells and whistles that make it so expensive. Your career search is not the place to begin to learn the intricacies of various software. Use what you know well. Borrow expertise from friends and colleagues, if they are willing to share their knowledge and skills with you. Buy the rest.

Do you find that there is more month left over at the end of the money? Many people do these days. So understand what you have already available and save buying new software until you really know what to do with it.

If you know a variety of software packages and computer languages, you have a rich resource to mine for presenting your résumé to the people most impressed by good résumés. Software will enable you to create a variety of résumé formats to dazzle and impress your potential employer. Just be sure you can duplicate what you demonstrate in your technology-driven résumé.

Getting a friend to do your résumé is not beneficial if in reading the résumé the potential employer gets the idea you know more about technology than you do. Just a word of warning to those who have slid along on the help of others: Get all the advice you can muster, but formulate your own résumé!

Those who are software literate may want to develop a demonstration disk that illustrates who you are. The information is the same as is on your traditional résumé, but looks different and is developed as a marketing tool. Its initial presentation is a disk (hardware) that is programmed, designed and developed by you. The disk is interactive with the reader (programming skills) and can be used in any compatible hardware (make sure of this before you send it). All of this identifies a very skilled programmer knowledgeable about marketing and technology.

Another option is to create a slide presentation that presents your credentials to a potential employer. PowerPoint in Windows Microsoft Office is but one package that gives a number of options to consider for a slide presentation of your résumé information.

Anyone who understands DOS and can work with it can translate a traditional résumé into ASCII text and put it on the Internet. There are many companies who look at the Internet each day to see who is advertising his or her skills with technology's help. Companies also advertise the job openings they have on the Internet so you have a chance to look at what is open, as well as a chance to screen the competition. You can access other people's résumés to compare against your own.

■ *INTERNET*

When you make your résumé available to others over the Internet it is possible to gather information about companies from their Web sites on the Internet. Business profiles usually run about one to one and a half pages long. You can also take a look and see what the comparable salaries are for the profession being pursued.

You also might want to consider creating a Web site on the Internet for yourself; begin with a creative screening of your résumé. This could later be developed into a consulting page for the entrepreneurs among you. If you are able, it is possible to create a multimedia presentation of your résumé.

Who would look for this type résumé? People in multimedia businesses. Who would be impressed by this? Most who saw it.

However, unless your résumé gets before the right decision-maker's eyes it may merely entertain, even create a good impression, but not help you get a job.

The problem with options is that distractions abound. Everything looks so exciting, and the completed copy appears easily accomplished, which is the sign of a professional. The challenges multiply, so what to do? Remember that your goal is to get the best possible job you can find for yourself in your chosen field.

◼ *CUSTOMIZED RÉSUMÉS*

First things first. The résumé should contain four parts: a *career objective or focus* (where are you going?), a *skills summary* (what can you do?), an *education summary* (what and where have you learned what you know?), and an *experience summary* (where have you worked and what have you done as work?). Also include your name, mailing address, e-mail address, telephone number, FAX number, and any other information that would help a potential employer reach you. Avoid using your present employer's phone, FAX, and e-mail on your résumé unless you are the only one who answers them.

All of the other types of résumés mentioned previously are the same résumé as the traditional one outlined in the preceding paragraph. Use only one résumé. Why get into these varieties of résumé presentation? To impress the reader. If you want to get a job with a multimedia company, then a multimedia presentation of your résumé information would impress company decision makers if they are looking for creative, innovative, imaginative, and intelligent types. Not every employer is!

If you want to get a job as a programmer, then it would be helpful if you could just present your résumé on a disk in any one of the ways discussed earlier. Does the job description or notice tell you that an employer is looking for creative and imaginative programmers with impeccable credentials and state-of-the-art skills in contemporary programming languages? If so, show them what you know with a programmed résumé, but go easy and light. You do not want to bore or overwhelm them. Your goal is to entice and intrigue decision makers to read the résumé.

If you do not have a clue about what to do, but you are sure you want to get into an exciting technology company, then float your résumé on the Internet using ASCII text. ASCII text removes all extra features such as underlining, boxing, margins, bold typeface, and so forth. So all employers can read is your objective, skill base, education, and experience. The résumé content had better be good. Remember, if you are filing your résumé on the Internet, use some keywords to describe yourself on the top line. These ASCII text résumés are filed by keywords, rather than your name, on the Internet. Some examples of keywords are B.A., *cum laude,* wordsmith, author, and creative brochure designer. Stay within forty-five to sixty characters for your keyword stripe.

Some other interesting ways to use the Internet access for job searching follow. Because of the rapid way the Internet and all the various Web and business sites change with technology advancements, some of these may no longer exist, but they are currently useful. Keep looking for even better and more creative ways to present your credentials to the right people who are looking for them. That is always your job.

Using a video presentation as a résumé substitute is risky business because so much is out of your control when the presentation is being viewed by the potential employer. First, you are not there to prepare the viewer. Second, you cannot see the reaction of the viewer. Third, you are not there to answer questions that may arise. Given these limitations, a video should be considered seriously only by a person who is extremely creative, who is really attractive and photogenic on video screen, who clearly enunciates so that no word can be misconstrued by the listener, and who demonstrates enthusiasm without looking blatantly like he or she is overacting.

First the viewer must ask for such a presentation. If the video arrives unannounced, it could give a bad impression of you as egotistical or suspiciously sophisticated. Is your major theater or acting? Get more advice. Can you afford a filming team? No amateurs should attempt this project alone. You can see this would mean a lot of money invested in a one-time show. It is possible, and it will impress some. The question is who it will impress. Do you have access to that person and did

If it sounds as though using a video-tape as a résumé substitute is being discouraged here, you got the message. It takes an extraordinarily talented person to make a dynamic impression the first time he or she is introduced to another. That video introduction is coming from a taped replay on video-tape. Are there places and people who can use this to advantage? Yes, but they are few and far between.

he or she ask for a video? This is not something to enter into lightly or without professional advice and counsel.

Chapter 3 has given you a new group of challenges to consider in the presentation of your résumé. If it goes to the Internet, you have twenty-four-hour access to decision makers who might review your résumé. Creative options of presenting résumé information on an interactive or demonstration disk allow programmers, or those who have programming skills, to show them off in a nontechnical environment.

The WWW itself presents new and growing options as technology improves and expands the communication of ideas.

The video option is identified with sufficient sinkholes and potholes to warn the amateur to beware and the professional to seek advice and counsel before attempting such a presentation.

Segment 1 has prepared you to recognize the help available to research information and create original formats. Recommendations are clear that you should make use of all three avenues of searching to get maximum coverage and twenty-four-hour visibility. And these are just the methods. Next, we cover the tools that will be needed to make the methods work effectively and efficiently.

Chapter 3 Challenges

Technology

1. Use the programmed disk to keep track of all the data you need to gather in this and future chapters. Locate the disk in appendix I and use it. You will save a lot of time and energy. The disk is a stand-alone, but it requires a Windows environment for you to use it.
2. Design a demonstration disk for your résumé. To whom would you send this? Why?
3. Develop a slide-show presentation of your résumé information. Who would use it to advantage? Where would you send it? Why? What distinguishes this approach from the others in your campaign?
4. If you are a programmer or can do some basic programming, design your own interactive disk for a résumé. First, determine why you want to do this. Keep your campaign goals in mind. Where will you send this disk résumé? Remember that the content remains the same as on your traditional version.
5. Float your ASCII Text résumé on the Internet for one week. Use a keyword stripe. Track the responses and results in some graphic format for your own record.
6. Chart a comparison of these different styles for delivering résumé information to the appropriate decision makers. Include choice of format and why it was chosen, describe the format style, focus beyond the résumé data delivery expectations of help or classification in your career field. What are you expecting your résumé to do, and who is most likely to see your résumé in a favorable light because of its format and style?

Traditional

1. Describe your ability to use the Internet and WWW and demonstrate how you would employ these two tools in your search campaign.
2. Describe your expertise at this moment with the hardware needed for your career search campaign.
3. Which software packages are you familiar enough with to use in your search? How would you take advantage of the opportunities in each package?
4. What four categories must be covered in every résumé, no matter the style or format?
5. Explain why a video presentation could be problematic for some career searchers.

Vocabulary

In a letter to a friend you want to tell about your career search process, explain how you will use the eleven italicized words in the following list to your advantage.

ASCII text	customized résumé	Internet	résumé
access	*dBase*	job openings	robots
best possible job	*DOS*	*keyword stripe*	salaries
business profiles	entrepreneurs	marketing tool	slide show
career objective	*education summary*	*Microsoft Office*	software
career search	e-mail	multimedia	video screen
competition	*experience summary*	*PowerPoint*	*visibility*
computer languages	FAX	programmer	*Visual Basic*
cover letters	hardware	program skills	Web site
credentials	interactive résumé		

Segment 2

TOOLS FOR JOB SEARCHING

■ *INTRODUCTION*

The focus of segment 2 is to raise your awareness that job searching is essentially a marketing exercise. To think of it as anything else is to be misdirected in your search and in some cases to be disappointed in the results. Marketing is hard work, but there is no better substitute if you want the best job you can secure for yourself in your new career.

The concepts covered in the four chapters of this segment are as follows: chapter 4, your readiness for the marketplace; chapter 5, your personal promotion factors; chapter 6, your individual market value with your new degree; and chapter 7, your visibility. These factors are all part of understanding your candidacy for a new position as a marketing pursuit. Marketing yourself is the best way to find the optimum opportunity for your accumulated education, experience, and skill base. This segment is about you and how you must prepare yourself to meet the challenges of the marketplace of your profession.

Chapter 4 analyzes ways for you to become aware of your personal readiness for the marketplace of choice. Candidates must know who they are (chapter 3), where they are headed (chapter 1), and who can best assist them to achieve their goals (chapter 2). Readiness includes education and experience that can be demonstrated by test, résumé, interview skills, critical thinking, creative thinking, and technical skills.

The next step is to develop a résumé that demonstrates your readiness for the market. Design this résumé with a clearly focused goal and identifiable support for the achievement of that goal. The résumé should be concisely composed, designed for the market of choice, and delivered to the prospective employer.

A clearly focused goal, objective, aim, view, target, design, or whatever you call it is one section where you have identified where you are going: What industry, what business, what field are you entering? Then illustrate your readiness by identifying what you bring to this new industry by way of skills, craft, proficiency, education, and experience. The information must be concisely arranged as one page of traditional text or an applicable number of screens for the same text available on disk or on-line. Your résumé must be designed for the market you wish to enter as stated in your original career focus statement. A good market design illustrates that you have thoroughly investigated the market and know what is acceptable, what will impress the reader, and what is considered important in the field.

Lastly, who is going to receive this missive? A personnel manager who does not necessarily know the field where the job is open may be the first reader of your résumé. Perhaps the manager of the department where the position is open will be the first reader of your résumé. It could be a new position for which there is not a precise fit defined in the company structure as yet, and an executive has been appointed to read your résumé. These are all problems that are essentially out of your control but within your understanding of how to approach by composing an appropriate cover letter to the right person in the company.

Your résumé must be appreciated by all levels of individuals in a company, as well as pleasing to the eye. Invite the reader to be interested in you more than other applicants. Compose a memorable résumé (sometimes made so by use of technology) to demonstrate your technical prowess at the same time you present a résumé.

There are a variety of formats to consider. These are outlined in the text. The disk accompanying the text is programmed for you to keep track of the data gathered from a variety of places in order to use it as needed. Use these data to formulate your résumé and remember the four areas as you create a traditional one-page résumé, keeping the four sections clearly visible to the potential readers.

The four areas include a career objective or focus statement, delineation of appropriate skills, education earned, and experience in the work world to support the objective. The résumé should also have your identification: name, mailing address, e-mail address, telephone numbers where you can be reached, and a FAX number, all listed together on the top or opening of the résumé.

Chapter 5 explains how to use your résumé effectively. The development of a formal market plan is begun in chapter 5 and continues later in segment 3. Interviewing preparation, purpose, evaluation, and assessment guides are outlined for the candidate to consider after each interview. Basic interviewing skills are also outlined, because they seem to be lacking in most people's awareness of business etiquette.

In chapter 6 you are assisted in analyzing the potential earning power that might be expected in the field of choice. This is based on the market value for similar positions at the time the search is conducted. The second factor is your personal earning power based on work history. Combining these factors sensibly will enable you to come up with a realistic salary range to consider for the position sought.

Negotiation skills are the best set of skills you can learn if you do not already possess them. Understand the negotiating edge you have as a recent graduate, an experienced worker in a field, a demonstrated learner about new technologies, and a creative and critical thinker, all of which are important when the negotiations begin in earnest.

No candidate can afford to be without a will to negotiate and the skills with which to do a good job.

The candidate is the only one negotiating for the candidate in each situation.

The negotiating background described in the chapter is based on John von Neumann's *Game Theory*, developed and researched in the nineteenth century. His theory has been adapted and adopted for this chapter, so candidates will have a handle on how to prepare for negotiations for themselves. This is an important set of skills for business. If you can demonstrate successful possession of these skills, it will be so noted by the employer.

Chapter 7 is devoted to your visibility. This visibility is first illustrated by the type, quality, and format of the résumé. Next the development of appropriate cover letters and their proper uses are explained. Interview etiquette is described often, because some candidates have not looked for a professional position recently. Etiquette is a professional skill and may be improved by practice. Behavior highlights are illustrated in order to continuously build good networking skills.

Segment 2 covers most of the marketing tools a candidate will need to prepare to meet the marketplace of choice. Readiness is outlined. Résumé formats are suggested. Marketing plans are developed. Interviews are approached from a wide variety of angles, from initial contact with employers to job acceptance. Know your potential value in the marketplace. It is half the job of negotiating.

Negotiating skills are explained. You are encouraged to make use of them, even if they are new to your arsenal of business skills. Cover letters are developed for the purpose the résumé is being sent. Business etiquette is also explained and expected to be used in all interviews. Networking skills are also illustrated, and practice is encouraged.

In this segment alone you will learn marketing, interviewing, negotiating, business, and networking skills. All these skills are needed for a thorough career search that will result in success. This chapter and the information disk will challenge you to use the best tools in job searching to advantage while applying the hard work that these established skills demonstrate in whoever possesses them.

LEARNING PROCESSES / SKILLS

MARKET READINESS

Degree
Career Goal/Focus
Primary Skills

RÉSUMÉ OUTLINE

Personal Identification
Career Objective
Skills Profile
Keyword Stripe
Education
Experience

RÉSUMÉ FORMAT OPTIONS

Chronological
Functional
Linear
Achievement
Performance

TECHNICAL FORMAT OPTIONS

ASCII Text
Internet Float

INTERNATIONAL FORMAT

Curriculum Vitae

Market readiness includes a wide variety of considerations. You must know and have contemplated all aspects of life, education, and work situations from which the skills, qualities, characteristics, and talents have been developed. It is assumed that having thoughtfully completed chapters 1, 2, and 3, your self-knowledge is contemporaneous with your age and competence.

Reformulate your information. You are now ready to think about your chosen field and what career title will best fit you. This is a new phase of your development and for many the beginning of a new career. Choices made and assessments evaluated about your readiness must be honest and fair. This is no place for an overactive sense of modesty. A realistic assessment of your values, skills, qualities, talent, education, and experience must be considered as the whole microcosm you are willing to share within a certain career field.

When are you ready to begin a career pursuit? After all is in place or soon to be in place and as many unseemly aspects or obstacles to achieve a new career have been removed. The tools you need are a clearly focused résumé, a market plan where that résumé would have meaning, a cover letter bank to use with potential employers, and a skills bank ready for action and improvement. When all of these items are ready, *you* are ready.

■ *RÉSUMÉ DEVELOPMENT*

The first task is to build a résumé. The purpose of a résumé is to highlight for the reader what you want to communicate about your preparedness for a new position, in this case a new career. Often people think of a résumé as a marketing tool to locate the dream job, and that by some magic formula the readers of these résumés will make a decision, sight unseen, because of something that attracts them while reading the résumé.

Wake up! The purpose of sending a résumé is to alert the decision maker that you would like an interview to discuss the job opportunity available in the business. The format of a résumé is varied, as we have seen in chapter 3. The content of the résumé needs to be fairly consistent to avoid dividing the attention of the reader. The résumé should clearly identify who created the résumé: name, mailing address, e-mail address, voice telephone numbers, and a FAX number. But remember that the real purpose of a résumé is to get an interview.

Career Objective

Next you need to clarify the goal of your search. Where are you headed? This is most clearly articulated by identifying two or three choices of industries: secondary education/robotics technology/microbiology, commercial aviation/computer sales and service/weather systems, or marketing/communication systems/history. The career fields or industries do not need to be related to each other.

The goal is to search in the first business area, from the viewpoint of the candidate, for about 100 interviews and if nothing satisfactory is discovered then move on to the second and third areas as needed. Sometimes candidates can put a string of industries together that fit well, such as elementary education/gymnastics/counseling or European history/French/organizational planning. The key is understanding what you want to venture into with regard to an industry. You do not have to have ever been employed in these industries. All you need is an interest in becoming a part of this new field.

The next phrase in the career objective is an identified list of three skill sets you currently possess and command in great abundance. These skills will be highlighted as already successfully accomplished. They describe the skills decision makers are looking to employ and highlight the skills you have accumulated over a lifetime. An employer does not want to hear about how much you intend to improve yourself on company time but what you can do for the company once employed.

This is the distinct and subtle difference that separates good résumés from poor ones. Skill words are "doing" words: manage, procure, supervise, program, teach, train, advise, plan, organize, analyze, and the list grows. The point here is that you must have these skills in great abundance if you highlight them in the career objective/focus. Then you can honestly say how these skills will help a business because you have used and developed them with success.

Next, illustrate for the employer how you think your three identified *skills* will enable the company to improve its bottom line, make better use of talent, have more access to customers, and solve or identify problems more accurately, quickly, and within stated guidelines. Translate exactly how your three skills identified earlier will convert to an improved business climate.

How do you know this? You have these skills in abundance, so you know what happens when you use them. These are not weak, new, or untried skills. The skills that you want to use in a new position are long-standing, tried, and proven. How will these skills make your new employer happy you came onboard?

Put on an employer or business owner's hat. Look at the chosen skills. One at a time list why, as an employer, you would want to employ someone with this particular skill. If you draw a blank then think about why the skill is helpful in general. Apply the same procedure to skills two and three. You now have a list of phrases to use when interviewers ask why they should hire you. These phrases are the result of exercising your skills. These phrases are your answers to interviewers' questions. Pick two or three of them as the strongest ones you have and close your career objective/focus statement with them.

EXAMPLE: Talent management skills could improve talent pool available for business, business planning skills might improve the work flow, supervisory skills would tighten the work schedule by removing downtime or waste, technical design skills would help in developing new products.

You can continue to list other opportunities. The critical decision here is for you to identify the best skills from your experience and education. Then transpose those skills into a business environment.

The **career objective** might look something like the following:

Scientific operations management/biochemistry/electronics technology, where skills in research, technical writing, and scientific talent supervision, coupled with hard work and a friendly team-player attitude will result in a company being able to take the lead in scientific developments, reach further and expand the customer base, and communicate effectively between customer needs and organizational capabilities to meet those needs, while observing business policies and guidelines.

Skills Profile

The support for this career objective lies in demonstrating just how skillful you are. These skills can be listed in columns or designated with appropriate modifiers if that is necessary to convey how skilled and qualified you are for the position desired. When you examine your rich skill base the deciding factor of whether to put this or that skill on the list is whether it supports one, two, or all three of your identified skills in the career objective.

EXAMPLE: If in the career objective you said your skills were blueprint reading, Spanish, and communication, how does that translate into helpful information for the decision maker to assess your qualifications? Use a similar translation.

Skills Profile Translation: Other Related Skills

Blueprint Reading	Computer DOS, 5.0 Hewlett Packard Printer hp 560 Macintosh, UNIX	Software Design Tools: Windows '95, TURBO C, C++, Microsoft Office Professional, ProComm Plus
Spanish	Beginning, intermediate, and advanced Spanish Spanish cultural history Six months study in Mexico City, 1998	
Communication	Published articles for technical magazines, Internet access, designed a Web page, public speaker	

Keyword Stripe

Keyword Stripe is a new designation that appears on ASCII text files. This is how the résumés are filed by Internet services. It might be something for you to think about using with the traditional résumé format. Place the keyword stripe at the top of the page. With actual ASCII text, string your identifying key words (no more than sixty-five characters).

EXAMPLE: Electronics, computer science, B.S. degree, 2 yr. experience.

Personal Identification

Jo Sampson	jpson@xxx.com
347 Main Street	513-555-7835 (h)
Hometown, Ohio 45112	513-555-8793 (o)
	531-555-8765 (FAX)

Since your education is recent, it follows the skills profile on the résumé. At times in your life when your education has receded a few years and you have more current experience, your experience would be listed first.

Education

When you list your education level and the field of your earned degree, it is sometimes meaningless to the reader because bachelor, master, and doctorate designations for educational levels are too various for anyone but the card cataloger or the dean who allows transfer credit to a new school to recognize and evaluate accurately. Explain what you studied and why it is significant in light of your career objective.

EXAMPLE: B.A. (Music Composition) Indiana University. Bloomington, Indiana (in progress).

Significant Courses (Theory)	**Important Labs**
Music theory (4 years)	Physics of sound lab 305
Orchestration	Instrument lessons (all instruments)
Chorus accompanist	Sight reading choral music

Projects
Senior year: Principal accompanist for choral groups
Senior project: *SSA Cantata for Women's Voices in G*
Project: *Trio in E♭ for Woodwinds*

Your studies have helped you gain certain skills that you now must sell. How did these courses assist you? Some courses were lectures where you learned about new skills. Others were laboratory courses where you practiced those new skills until they become second nature to you. Throughout your term of study there were projects you completed for certain courses. Organize the most significant of these educational experiences in light of the three skills you identified in the career objective.

EXAMPLE: B.S. (Speech Therapy) Open Heads College. Down the Road, Iowa.

Significant Courses		**Important Laboratory Courses**
Physio-psychology	PSYC305	Hearing laboratory assignments
Anatomy	MED254	Anatomy laboratory L254
Principles of management	MGMT303	Management laboratory L303
Computer applications	COMP101	Computer laboratory L101

Projects	**Honors**
Community-development project	President's list (4 years)
School-site supervised therapy	Dean's list (4 years)
Evaluation tool development for	Phi Beta Kappa
children with hearing-deficit problems	

When you say what was significant or important about your course work and your laboratory experiences you give a window of insight for the potential employer to assess your readiness for the open position. When you cite various projects you demonstrate how you have used the theory and practice together. This helps a stranger evaluate you more accurately and says more than your earned degree focus and the college from which you graduated. The rationale for selection is always how supportive these educational experiences were to your identified skill base in the career objective.

Experience

Next follows your experience. This usually includes your last two jobs. They can be jobs you held while you were going to school. A collection of customer service jobs with several companies can be listed as one job. There could be a job you would rather have on your résumé from before you went to school. Entry-level candidates usually have their jobs during college, while midlevel candidates may have had better and more powerful work experience before they decided to go back to school for a degree.

EXAMPLE:

Customer Service. Various gas stations and restaurants in the Delmarva area.

Responsibilities included meeting customer needs, solving customer problems, procuring supplies in timely fashion, closing the register, taking deposits to the bank, opening and closing the operation. (1996–Present)

Department Manager. Saks Fifth Avenue Department Stores. Kansas City, Missouri.

Responsibilities included hiring and training individuals for the department, assessing and evaluating personnel for promotion, submitting and maintaining an annual budget for the department, purchasing merchandise for the department, and handling customer complaints. (1993–1996)

Often candidates will want to give the whole history of work back to baby-sitting in the fifth grade. The potential employer is only interested in what you have done recently, whether you are a steady worker, and that there is enough information for referral calls to present and former employers. Remember that this is not your life story but a reference point for a stranger to make an assessment of your potential to fill a vacancy in the business.

The résumé should be sharply focused, accurately informative, inviting to read, and clearly representative of your best qualifications for the position you want. The keyword stripe is optional on the traditional résumé but mandatory on any résumé that travels the Internet.

The content should be arranged so that the reader can easily find the career objective or career focus (where is the candidate going?), a skills profile (what does the candidate know how to do?), an education section (what does the candidate have by way of educational support for the skills listed in the career objective and on the skills profile?), and finally what experience the candidate brings to support the skills being highlighted on the résumé. The arrangement of these sections is a personal and professional matter. Some suggestions follow about format.

There are a variety of résumé books on the market that are devoted to the various ways one can arrange the information on a page or on a screen. Here are a few ideas. Select what fits you, looks visually inviting on the page or screen, and contains the material highlighted in the previous paragraph. They will include

- Chronological résumé
- Functional résumé
- Linear résumé
- Achievement résumé
- Performance résumé
- ASCII text format for computer screens
- Disk arrangements for those who can program their own disks

■ *RÉSUMÉ FORMAT OPTIONS*

Chronological Résumé

The chronological résumé is the oldest of the traditional résumé formats. It is usually used by someone who wants to stay in the same field. The accent is on the career goal or focus, and the skills profile, education, and experience sections are supportive of the three skills highlighted in the career focus. Sometimes experience precedes education on this résumé, because experience is the most recent of the two. Stress accomplishments and professional affiliations on one page. Remember, it is your story.

Functional Résumé

The functional résumé is used when entering a new field or moving to a new geographical location. This résumé should highlight functional skills in light of a goal statement. The accent is on the career objective, which identifies three areas of interest and draws focus to three specific skills. The skills profile, education, and experience segments support the three skills. Build additional skills profile for support of the three identified skills. The keyword stripe is helpful to highlight your identified skill base. This would be the résumé of a published author, a person with strong management background, a developer/designer/inventor of software, a recent graduate, and so forth.

Linear Résumé

The linear résumé is a 1990s version of a chronological résumé that includes a summations paragraph, rather than a career objective/focus statement, but serves the same purpose. List qualifications or skills on single lines with bullets for visual impact. In the employment section accent position titles, job descriptions, and lists of achievements. Education criteria close this résumé.

Achievement Résumé

The achievement résumé is targeted, with a clearly identified and sharply focused career objective/focus statement. Rather than a background summary, build a short description of the job target. Supportive data include capabilities, skills, and achievements. Close this résumé with employment history and education credentials.

Performance Résumé

The performance résumé highlights a candidate's highest performance level reached so far in the career track. The keyword stripe is helpful here. The accent is on accomplishments in the field, concisely stated. The detail is descriptive of what skills are necessary to perform at that level. Build the educational and experiential support for the identified skills profile and the keyword stripe. Published authors, people with concentrated career data in midlevel to senior management, inventors, creators and designers of software products, developers of hardware improvements, and similar candidates are most likely to use the performance résumé.

■ *TECHNICAL RÉSUMÉ OPTIONS*

Internet

People looking for jobs on the Internet must know how to translate their traditional text résumé to an ASCII text format. The reason for this translation is that ASCII text is the simplest code in the technology. It can be sent to various hardware and therefore may reach a wide variety of people with varying software capabilities, as well as company equipment. The simplest text is an ASCII text file. Remember that the format is the only difference here; the content remains the same. The keyword stripe belongs at the top of the page as the first bit of information available; do not use a keyword stripe label.

The accent is on the career objective; connect the skills profile, education, and experience to support the three skills highlighted in the career objective. Build more skills into the skills profile to expand your skill base profile. This ASCII text résumé can be sent immediately to the Internet provided you have access. This type of résumé format is for people who are looking for technical jobs or jobs with technology companies. The résumé floats on the Internet twenty-four hours a day and is accessible by anyone who has Internet connection.

In all cases when you are using the Internet, ASCII text files, FTPs, an on-line service or bulletin board service, software, or binary files, read the manual for how to use these options. When using e-mail, know what the e-mail system you are using can do by reading the manual. E-mail systems are all different in their capabilities.

Candidates looking for jobs and employers looking for talented candidates meet for twenty-four hours a day on the Internet. Many schools make Internet access possible for all students or those who wish to use it. Increasing numbers of businesses also have access to the Internet for the business uses of their employees.

If you wish to have your own personal account, use one of the commercial services to access the Internet. These include America Online, Prodigy, Genie, Netscape, and others. Investigate and evaluate carefully for the best buy. The charges are different from company to company.

Once you have Internet access, you need to know a little about how a modem works (and that is all you need to know about the hardware). The software depends on what you are using. For research purposes you can use the Internet to read business profiles, see comparable résumés to yours, read job openings, select the salary comparison charts, and float your résumé on the Internet. Most Internet services will make your résumé available for twenty-four hours a day if you wish.

ASCII Text

Take your traditional text résumé and convert it to ASCII text. Two reasons for ASCII text are that all receivers may not be able to see what you send unless it is in ASCII format. This is a critical consideration. Second, anything from the WWW will be in HTML format and will not download without some machine language riddled throughout your résumé. Take charge of your résumé; file it in ASCII text so it will download properly.

Optical Character Recognition

Some employers use scanners and optical character recognition (OCR) software to select which résumés sent through land mail will receive consideration. Often this is used to screen quickly for the best candidates. Others use the keyword search function to select the best ASCII text résumés on-line. You must be prepared for all options and take advantage of the variety technology affords you. But know to whom you are sending your résumé, for what purpose, and what you want your "résumé to say about YOU, other than what it reads about you!"

■ *INTERNATIONAL RÉSUMÉS*

Curriculum Vitae

Curriculum Vitae, sometimes shortened to *Vitae,* is a Latin term that literally means life course. Originally the Curriculum Vitae was used in academic settings where new professors were expected to reveal their levels of education, positions held at which universities, published books and articles in scholarly journals, honors they may have won as scholars, scientists, doctors, and other high-profile achievers.

Today these Vitae are preferred in Europe. They usually run six to eight pages in length, depending on the achievements of the individual. American higher education institutions still require some form of this Curriculum Vitae, as do some government jobs, diplomatic positions, and military brass appointments. In Japan there is a special Curriculum Vitae that candidates for positions are expected to use. England has a suggested form for the Curriculum Vitae. Candidates are expected to make use of these formats in England and some countries on the continent.

If applying for a position in a non-English-speaking country, have your résumé translated into the native language of that country on one side of the résumé and in English on the other side. Do the same with any business cards you intend to use. For most positions in the American business world, though, the one-page résumé is preferred by decision makers.

Chapter 4 has highlighted the first tool necessary in marketing yourself in the field of your choice. What makes a visually exciting résumé is often in the eye of the creator and the beholder. However, there are some standards that should be observed. First, whatever is on the résumé should be spelled correctly, and no English usage errors are tolerated.

Second, the résumé must have four easily identifiable sections where information can be gleaned at a glance. These are career objective, skills profile, education, and experience. For those who wish, a keyword stripe is a focused summary that hurried readers appreciate. Your name, mailing address, e-mail address, voice telephone numbers, and FAX numbers should be available for the decision maker to reach you if he or she has questions or wants to see you.

Third, expectations in each of these categories are detailed and examples given. There is no résumé example per se because the résumé is your portrait of yourself and your readiness for the market. Therefore, it should look professional and unique.

Fourth, there are different ways to communicate your résumé content to a decision maker. Regardless of whether you use a traditional format on one printed page, are able to develop and design an interactive disk format, or can manage a video presentation, your résumé must be clear, concise, and look professional from all aspects.

Your résumé says more about you than your résumé says!

Chapter 4 Challenges

Technological

1. Design a résumé and put the best copy on the accompanying disk for safekeeping.
2. Design a graphic to make *Game Theory* and negotiations clear to yourself. What are the important values for you? Prioritize their relationships to each other. Work out the chart so you can use it.

3. Use the cover letter options on the disk, as well as those described in this chapter, to your advantage. You do not have to have a template to write a cover letter. The templates are designed to help you formulate a good business letter. You are responsible for the content.
4. Illustrate a calendar where you have scheduled thirty to thirty-five interviews a week. Carry out the calendar. What did you learn?
5. Search the Internet for salary potential in your chosen field. Chart the results. Save this information and compare it with your market value determined in chapter 6.
6. Use the disk in appendix I to track your data and your progress. Analyze weekly for insight and some wisdom about your process and strategy.

Traditional

1. Outline the tools you need for a market search.
2. Describe your attitude going into a job search campaign.
3. List the three most difficult questions you think will be asked of you in an interview. Answer each of these questions three different ways. Practice.
4. Explain *Game Theory,* as it is applied to negotiations, to a classmate.
5. Gather in small groups and read, compare, critique, and make suggestions for improvement for each member's career objective/focus, skills profile, education, and experience statements. Try to improve each one's work.

Vocabulary

Select the words that are related to résumé and formulate them into a crossword puzzle for a member of your support group or your classmates. Include a list of definitions for the columns and rows on the puzzle.

achievement	etiquette	networking
ASCII text	experience	on-line service
BBS	FAX	performance
binary files	FTPs	personal earnings
calendars	functional	proficiency
candidate	*Game Theory*	qualities
career focus	interactive disks	readiness
career objective	Internet	résumé
chronological	interviews	salary
computer screens	job search	skills profile
contacts	keyword stripe	slide presentations
creative thinking	leads	strategic plans
critical thinking	linear	talent
decision makers	marketing	techniques
demo disks	market design	visibility
education	market value	Web page
e-mail	negotiate	

Chapter 5

CANDIDATE PROMOTION

LEARNING OBJECTIVES

After you study this chapter, you should be able to

- Produce a professional résumé that will get you an interview and make it easy for you to communicate with your interviewer about your chosen career field.
- Combine the best art of an interview, conversation style, with the clearest presentation of ideas about your readiness for a career position.
- Use your résumé as a tool to gain access to an interviewer rather than as a marketing device that works by itself to gain you access.
- Set standards for your interviewing techniques and style.

- Have a conversational interviewing style.
- Build a clear and adequate approach to your marketing campaign.
- Synthesize your understanding of the company's procedures and policies to use when negotiating compensation.
- Practice and develop great interviewing skills.
- Distinguish and choose selectively among the different styles and purposes for interviews.
- Maximize what is available to assist you in reaching your marketing campaign goals.

LEARNING PROCESSES / SKILLS

INTERVIEWS

Science
Art
Conversation

RÉSUMÉ USE

Industries
Companies of Interest
Human Resources Professionals
Interview Tool

MARKETING PLAN

Campaign Time Line
Numbers Game
Interviews
Informational Interviews
Job Interviews

Negotiation Interviews
Interview Skills
Decision Making

SKILLS

Conversational
Personal Interaction
Sensitivity
Composure
Time Management
Business Manner
Prioritizing
Decision Making
Planning
Organizing
Self-Knowledge

Chapter 5 is dedicated to putting your own promotion uppermost in your thoughts and your pursuit of selected employment. You have a résumé, and this chapter will describe various ways you can get your résumé before the right pair of eyes.

If your résumé is not seen by the right person, it makes little difference how hard you have worked to produce an effective résumé.

Secondly, a marketing plan must be outlined so you have an organizational frame from which to work toward your goal. You have the substance and you must now plan for the best promotion of that substance—you. Who needs to know about you? When do they need to know about you? From whom might they hear about you? Who do you know in the industry or career field of your choice? What is the plan?

The way to handle interview situations best is to be prepared. You must know the company, its history, its main contributions to the economy and its field, and where it might be located in relation to its peers/competitors. You need to know who in the organization is the best contact for you. Who would know the most about what you have to say about yourself and your preparation for a given career field?

■ *INTERVIEWS*

It is in the interview that you are accepted or rejected. You can have an exquisite résumé that might be the envy of all who see it and have a simply awful personality. In today's world you will not get the job. There are too many qualified people who are nice to know, work comfortably with teams and in groups, freely share their information and knowledge with others, and are considerate and friendly people.

Interviewing is about questions: Questions you have and the employer has that are exchanged in a conversational style. An interview is not a test of your knowledge. It is a conversation between two people who have similar interests about business, science, education, or any other fields. Can you carry on a conversation that includes answers to questions about you and your preparation to enter a career field? Do you have questions about a company's policies, marketing position, economic viability, human resources procedures, culture, and so on? You both have much to discuss. Interviewing is a skillful process for both sides. More and more interviewers are aware of their responsibilities while interviewing. Laws regulate what you can be asked in an interview. Candidates are also becoming aware of their rights, their privacy, and questions that might cross over into privacy issues (see appendix E).

Interviewing is a science and an art. It only improves with practice. This marketing plan is built so that you begin interviewing where you are comfortable and gradually move to more and more sensitive levels of interviewing. There is no substitute for actually interviewing. Your self-esteem is on the line.

You reveal who you are in an interview by the way you speak, the way you move, the questions you ask, the research you have or have not done, and the way you look. Your friendliness, enthusiasm, and behavior tell an interviewer more about you than you can say in the interview or the employer can read on your résumé. In this case, you say more than the interviewer asks of you by demonstrating who you are through your behavior in the interview.

■ *RÉSUMÉ USE*

Using the résumé skillfully, designing an adequate marketing plan, and preparing for the interview questions and answers from your side, as well as from the interviewer's side, are all skills and part of the art of good interviewing. This is where the process has led you and where you must be prepared for the challenges, because there will be many.

Now that you have your résumé ready, where will you send it? Return to your research sources and identify companies and industries that are of interest to you. Your first search is for companies that are in the industry you identified in the career objective.

EXAMPLE: If you said accounting, you need to identify the SIC for accounting and then search by code numbers for companies who do nothing but accounting, companies that use computerized accounting methods, businesses that create software for accounting/bookkeeping systems, companies that demonstrate or teach accounting methods and software, companies that have large bookkeeping/accounting departments, and others who are significantly involved in accounting methods and practice. At this time, keep your eyes on the classified sections of your local newspaper because there are almost always positions open for accountants.

If you indicated business administration, then you need to research companies in need of business degrees for their positions. There will also be a good number of want ads in the classified section of your local paper. You may have written Engineering. If so, move toward the SIC, find the number, and search by code in geographical sections of business directories for a match between what companies do and what you want to do. Do not neglect the "Business Profiles" of InfoTrac, the "Business Articles" using ProQuest, or the Internet using a keyword search.

Earlier we noted that résumés are not marketing devices but tools whereby you can get an interview. You must sell yourself in the interview. No company hires a résumé. They all want to see you, talk with you, get a feel for how you think, how you react to professional situations, how you talk about your chosen profession, and similar issues. Where your résumé goes depends on you and who you want to see your résumé.

In your research of companies, locate the individual at the appropriate level in the organization whom you have discerned would have similar professional interests to yours, be aware of the industry needs, and be able to evaluate your academic preparation and work experience in light of the business need.

Some candidates investigate at the wrong level and often interview with human resources personnel first. These people may not understand what the intricacies of the position require of the candidates.

In most companies where there is an identified human resources department, the employees in this department are most versed about insurance packages and benefits, employee 401K pension plans, internal conflict-resolution policies, employee unrest resolution, and sometimes continued training options in situations like sexual harassment issues, general legal issues, broad areas that affect employees' behavior, and corporate responsibilities for their employees' behavior. They are not necessarily well versed on your individual capabilities as a computer programmer in fourth-generation languages.

Well-run companies will have the human resources person and the manager looking to fill an open position confer on the requirements and the interviewing chores surrounding a new hire.

When you are doing research in the field, you need to talk with people who are most likely to hire someone like you for a position in the department. This does not mean that there is a position open at the time you write to them, but they may be willing to talk with you. You cannot get enough information and counsel while in an active search mode.

Think carefully about whom you want to interview concerning the field you have prepared to enter. You need information from this level of person in your field to understand what hiring practices are and why they are the way they are from this individual decision maker's standpoint.

There will be a variety of information you can get at this level, and there is no other way to get it than by interviewing. Your résumé begins this process. Where are you going to send it? By what method are you going to communicate the résumé information? What follow-up will be necessary after you have sent the résumé?

The résumé is a tool to get an interview and sometimes a tool to begin a business conversation between two strangers about a field of common interest to both of them. Use the tool widely. The more you use it, the more confident you will become regarding its uses and the better you will become at articulating answers to questions interviewers may have about various items on your résumé. You will notice that the résumé is soon put aside during the interview, because it has accomplished its work. You are interviewing the person you wanted to see. Do a good job. Your résumé did its work.

■ *MARKETING PLAN*

Building an appropriate marketing plan takes time and deserves careful consideration and planning on your part, but you must remember that it is not the entire strategy. Perspective is of great value here. What do you have time to do and how effectively can you accomplish the tasks?

The marketing plan consists of everything from completion of the résumé to negotiating the best deal you can make with a future employer. Marketing is something you must do constantly or you will not find the best offer for yourself. You will find offers within the first few days or weeks of your specified campaign, but you will not find the best offer until you have completed your marketing plan.

The process is a numbers game and the more people you see in the right fields and at the appropriate levels within organizations, the more quickly you will have real options to consider.

The marketing campaign consists of about eight to ten weeks of intensive, everyday interviewing or twelve to fifteen weeks of interviewing at least two to five times a day.

You can begin the gradual interviewing process while you are still in school. This means planning your time and curtailing your extra activities so that you will have about five interviews a week while completing projects, studying for exams, and managing the general hustle and bustle of a graduating term.

These interviews should be at the personal level with people you know—friends, relatives, college cronies, and business associates with whom you may be working. Your goal for these interviews is to make sure that people understand what you are hoping to gain in a job and why you want their help. Accept graciously whatever time and leads they have to share with you.

Within this time you can also interview peer-level personnel in the field of your choice. Your goal here is to make sure you understand from peers what is happening in the field from their perspective. This will soon be your perspective, so listen carefully. These people get paid regularly for doing what you want to do: pay attention to them.

This is the only group, by the way, with whom you might discuss salary options. This is true because these people will be the least likely to be in a situation to hire you this first time. It is significant because your negotiation process cannot be contaminated by your having inadvertently raised the salary issue before negotiation time.

These people are basically strangers to you. You have uncovered who they are by investigating companies where you think this level of employee may be hired. The receptionist has given you the name of the individual, and you have followed with a letter asking him or her for an interview. You have also included a copy of your résumé so the interviewer can see that you are a serious candidate looking for information. This is the beginning of your networking group.

By the time you have graduated you will have a lead list of prospects that will allow you to do serious interviewing of twenty interviews a week in the field of your choice. Do this for six weeks and you will have a wealth of opportunities from which to choose.

You may say that you will find a job earlier than that. You might. But with what do you have to compare it? The point of any marketing campaign is to make the product available everywhere and to everyone who might be interested. This is what you must do before you can say that the possibility of finding any better options than you have so far is pretty slim. You may say, "I think offer X is the first one I would like to negotiate to a finish, and if that does not work then I'll go to offer Y." Without an extensive campaign of six weeks in a crowded market you would not have offer Y.

A choice of one out of one is no choice.

■ *MARKETING CAMPAIGN*

Interviews during this intense marketing period that we will call the marketing campaign are usually of some variety and degree level. First, information interviews begin with inquiry—you are looking for information and advice. This advice can help you build information in your field and also identify others in the field whom you should know and who should know you.

Second, these interviews turn into job interviews on the spot. A series of interviews follow whereby you let the company know that you are interested. Be sure the potential employer answers all your questions about the company and the position. This could lead to six or ten interviews. It all depends on how deeply you want to go with the process. Interestingly enough, you are in the driver's seat here.

These interviews are about making the job so clear to you that you see yourself functioning in it successfully. You have no more questions about the job, its importance to the company, where it will lead you, training you might need to begin the job, coworkers, or company culture. You may even have met the manager of the department. You have no more questions. You are ready to negotiate.

■ *NEGOTIATION*

You have all your questions answered, the company has all its references, and you are still a top candidate for the position. However, you are not quite ready to negotiate and be fair to yourself. You need more information. The next set of interviews is about negotiation.

The company negotiator holds all the cards and has all the answers. Since this is a negotiating session you will find that the company negotiator will answer all your questions happily but will not introduce any other information. If you forget to ask, you have missing pieces when you come to the table to negotiate for real. So plan carefully.

Negotiation Interview #1

The first negotiation interview is to find all you can in order to negotiate competently. Begin this session with a summary of everything you understand about the job so far: your title, responsibilities, hours, teammates, supervisor, chances for moving into another position, the time frame of promotions, and what you have previously discussed. Then ask if you have misunderstood anything or misrepresented the company's position about the summary. If all is agreeable, then you are ready to begin the negotiating process. This means finding out the following by asking; no assumptions are allowed.

1. What is the salary range? How often or how soon will there be a review of your work? When does the second year salary begin? (Usually at your first-year anniversary, but ask.)
2. What are the dimensions of the benefits package? Usually there will be three major areas: insurance coverage, education benefits, and time off. Your purpose is to understand the limits and ramifications of the firm's policies in each of these areas. It is important for you to know why it offers what it does so that you will be in a better position to negotiate later. You also need to know the financial limits of these benefits. Ask everything; do not assume anything.
3. What are the remuneration policies if you are expected to use your own money in the pursuit of your job duties? How is this remuneration handled? Why is the policy the way it is? Do not be timid. You need these answers.
4. What other benefits are available and when would they become available to you? Some possibilities are pensions, bonuses, stock options, access to box seats at sports or cultural functions where the organization has box seats, outplacement costs if you are released through no fault of your own or your performance, and the indigenous benefits that are available (benefits that accrue because of the position you hold or services that the company provides to its customers may be provided to its employees at reduced rates or no cost).
5. What are the company policies about having to move your family and worldly goods in order to accept the position? What is the policy about remuneration of interviewing expenses for you, house-hunting trips for you and your partner, moving expenses, and placement needs for a spouse? How are these reimbursements handled?

Once you are sure you thoroughly understand the salary and benefits packages and how you are going to be compensated when you assume the new position, then you are ready to think about these issues and plan for session two of negotiation interviews.

Chapter 5 has covered the "slippery slope" for new job searchers. Look at the use you want to make of your well-designed résumé. Does it communicate what you want it to say and does it look the way you want it to look? Ask someone else to read it and tell you what it says about you in its content and appearance.

The marketing plan must be concise and tight. Do your lead-up interviewing for support and information while you are still in school. Then from your pack of leads begin your decision-maker interviewing as quickly as you can by scheduling at least twenty interviews a week. Interweave negotiating interviews as they present themselves throughout your campaign. The campaign is six to eight weeks in duration.

■ *INTERVIEW SKILLS*

Interviews are conversations. However, they need preparation because the conversation occurs between two strangers interested in the same professional field. Never approach an interview without knowledge about the company, the job, or the company's place in the economy.

Interviewing skills are numerous. They include conversational skills, personal interactive ability, sensitivity, knowledge, composure, peer interaction (in some cases), planning, organization, time management, prioritizing, and so forth. These skills alone will make you a better employee.

Decision makers are looking for more than someone who can use a computer, add up a column of figures, or talk a blue streak. They are always measuring you in ways you cannot comprehend at the moment, but you know you have made an impression. Just as first impressions never get a second chance, unknown impressions can dog you through your career. Self-knowledge is vital.

Ask, so as not to assume, how you were perceived in an interview when all is said and done. You will learn a lot about yourself—and it is valuable self-knowledge you should have.

The candidate promotes self. This must be so. There are no shortcuts to the best job possible. Detailed campaign issues must be met effectively and on time. Learning too late that your résumé has a glaring spelling error it not good enough. Learn from others.

Most will be happy to give you an evaluation if you really want one. Decision makers, for the most part, are always evaluating someone—employees, candidates for employment, recruits, personnel aspiring for promotions, peers, and their supervisors. For the most part they are pretty good at it, and you could benefit from what they have observed.

You cannot be thin-skinned about criticism, and you cannot take the criticisms personally. This is a lesson learned the hard way by some candidates. If you do not want the criticism, do not ask for it. However, you are impoverished without it.

Chapter 5 Challenges

Technological

1. Chart the purposes of the first negotiation interview.
2. Design a flowchart that illustrates the passage of your résumé from you to its intended reader.
3. Design a six-week marketing campaign on a calendar. Use it faithfully to the end. What have you learned about yourself and the job market?
4. Take the feedback you get from interviewers and chart it against how you think you did in the interviews. After five of these interviews, compare notes. What kind of pattern do you see?

Traditional

1. What is your stance in an interview? How is an interview different from a test?
2. What questions have you outlined for yourself to ask regarding policies, procedures, reputation, competition, legal dimensions, and products or services?
3. Describe the purpose and function of a résumé in an interview.
4. What do you understand human resources personnel's role to be in job interviewing?
5. Why do you need more information when all your questions about the job, the company, the industry, and the position you will fill have been answered? What questions are still left in the air? How will you approach them?
6. How would you set up criteria for yourself to measure your performance in interviews? What do you expect of yourself? If you ask the interviewer to evaluate your performance in the interview, what criteria will you expect to be used? Figure out a way to compare the interviewer's assessment with your preconceived criteria. What does it tell you about your style?
7. Explain how you would promote yourself in a search campaign. What avenues could you use to advantage? What tools would help you succeed?

Vocabulary

Create an interview dialogue you might have with a personnel officer about an open position for which you are well suited. Use as many appropriate words from this chapter as your instructor suggests or that you feel will work best.

benefits	InfoTrac	pension plans	references
best job possible	insurance	personality	remuneration
campaign	interaction	planning	résumé
composure	Internet	policies	salary
conversation	interview	prioritizing	self-esteem
criticism	job duties	procedures	self-knowledge
economy	marketing plan	promotion	sexual harassment
education	negotiate	ProQuest	SIC
human resources	outplacement	prospects	viability
indigenous	peers	reimbursements	401K plan

Chapter 6

MARKET VALUE

LEARNING OBJECTIVES

After you study this chapter, you should be able to

- Comprehend and evaluate your place and market value in the career field of your choice.
- Bring self-confidence to bear on your negotiating skills.
- Determine market value using real-life assessments and figures.
- Use placement offices carefully and knowledgeably.
- Gather correct figures from reliable resources.
- Determine your personal job acceptance criteria before you have that first interview.

- Use the market value determination form to help you figure an appropriate range for your salary limits.
- Research the cost of living where you plan to live and work. Compare these figures with where you are now living.
- Negotiate a good salary and adequate benefits package for yourself.
- Negotiate interviewing and house-hunting expenses if these are available as an option or policy.
- Negotiate trailing-spouse benefits implied in your choice and potential move.

LEARNING PROCESSES / SKILLS

SKILLS

Negotiations
Research
Evaluation
Marketplace Value
Interviewing
Job Acceptance Criteria
Cost of Living Comparisons
Determine Benefits Package Value
Game Theory

PERSONAL MARKET VALUE

Actual Market Value
Degree Value
Personal Earnings Value
Cost of Living

RELIABLE RESEARCH

Career Placement Agencies
Graduate Placement
Chambers of Commerce
Peer Interviews

NEGOTIATIONS

Self-Knowledge
Knowledge of Economy
Game Theory
Benefits Package
Trailing-Spouse Benefits
Turndown Point
Self-Esteem
Presentation

Chapter 6 is devoted to helping career candidates correctly assess their readiness for the market in terms of probable salary ranges. Knowing one's market value is crucial to interviewing for the best position, meeting the best contacts, and presenting your accomplishments, education, experience, talent, and skills in the best light to a total stranger. Knowing your market value will enable you to sort through the jobs available for appropriateness and to seek open positions.

There is also a certain amount of self-confidence that comes from knowing what others consider your value and what you know you have earned. Assessing the latest six months of earning power will illustrate what you have earned. Knowing what your degree is worth will illustrate the value others put on your effort as signified by your degree.

Know how to negotiate for yourself. Everyone can learn this set of skills. But learning the skills and practicing the skills are two different things. You can read books, listen to tapes, and take advice from friends and associates about how to play the piano. However, until you take that knowledge and actually apply it to the instrument you will never succeed.

The same is true of negotiating skills. There are innumerable titles in bookstores and libraries from which you might select the knowledge of how to negotiate. Reading these books will not help you negotiate any better if you have not tried some of the principles in everyday life. You get better at negotiating the same way you get better at interviewing—through practice.

The negotiator for the company has much experience, because the skills are needed every time a new person is hired, a new vendor is selected, equipment is purchased, and services are contracted. If you can negotiate well on behalf of yourself the business will value that skill in you for future positions with it.

Continue to negotiate, evaluate your performance, learn from your mistakes, listen to the advice of good negotiators, and go back to those books and tapes and compare how you are doing. The business world prizes negotiating skills. If they can be demonstrated during your interviews, the negotiating skills will hold you in good repute with the negotiator.

This chapter on market value is critical because of the skills learned and the impact of using those skills while negotiating your compensation. First, you must have a reasonable range for your salary that has been developed in light of the immediate compensation options in the chosen field and the earning value previously accumulated in the workplace. Considering these segments will enable you to arrive at a clear, fair, and equitable range of compensation. Testing it in the real market is the second step.

Knowing your market value will help in the negotiating or final stages of the interviewing process. Being able to negotiate confidently for yourself is a skill that all business decision makers appreciate. You will impress them if you are confident, aware of the marketplace value for your degree and skills, and can negotiate clearly a good bargain as compensation for the exchange of your skills, knowledge, degree, experience, and talent.

You continue to build a skill base. This chapter's skills of projecting your worth in the marketplace of the moment, coupled with negotiating skills that will enable you to make the best possible deal, all continue to add to your job searching tools.

■ MARKET VALUE DETERMINATION

Begin with a method to decide what you might be worth in the marketplace. You now have a new degree, new knowledge, and new skills, coupled with whatever skills you had before earning the degree. Divide your consideration into two sections. The first will concentrate on the market at the time you are entering it, and the second will look at your personal earnings history up to the moment of graduation.

As you are entering the job market after graduation, it is important to know what levels of salary are available for your career interests. You can determine this by taking a look at the journals and periodicals published where you live or plan to live. Ads are a good source for salary ranges, but the listing of a salary or salary range is becoming less and less available in print because most companies expect candidates to negotiate a salary. However there are a few so look at them and record them over the six-month period before graduation.

Placement agencies that profess they have jobs for you can be considered, but be careful. No ethical placement agency would ask for a fee from you before service is given. All agencies work for companies; they do not work for you. This is true no matter what sales pitch they give you. So you should not have to pay them before they deliver the job you want.

Do they deliver? Sometimes, but usually not exactly as you hoped the job would be. You are the best searcher for a new position. Only you know what you really want. The agency wants to fill a position because then it gets paid by the company hiring you. It has no special interest in finding you the ideal position. Are they helpful? Some are, most are not. How can you tell the difference? Listen to what they say when you hear their ads, and question and interview them carefully before you ask for their help.

Placement agencies need to be selected by you after interviewing several managers of different agencies. You need to know their policies of placement, where the records of your contract are held, and the relationship they have to the field of your interest. No agency can adequately serve all fields in today's business world.

If you are prepared to be a teacher, select an agency that places teachers on a regular basis. If you are an electronics or computer science engineer, then use an agency that specializes in electronics and computer science. If you are a historian, then find an agency that specializes in placing academics. If you are an accountant, go to a accounting placement agency. Focus and be as careful about the placement agency as you were about selecting the degree you wanted to earn from the college you wanted to attend.

The graduate-placement office in your school functions as a placement agency on your behalf. Know what it is willing to do for you and take advantage of the services available. If the graduate-placement office is an active one, it more than likely keeps records so you can check on the value of your degree from the school.

National and regional statistics on employment subjects are available from the chamber of commerce in your area. The U.S. Department of Labor keeps statistics about who is hired, where they are hired, for what salaries they are hired, and the titles of the positions for which they are hired. This is but a small piece of the information.

Finally, part of your informational interviewing is with people who would be your peers in the field of your choice. One of the questions you can ask these individuals is what salary range they feel would be appropriate for you at this time in your career and in the economy of your career field. You should have a fairly good picture after you have asked five or six people about this issue. Total and average this information into a market value range.

Next look at your pay stubs and record the figures for earnings at the last job you had. If you have no current job, then take a look at the last meaningful job you held. Make some adjustment for inflation. If the job was a part-time job, calculate the figures as though they were paid on a full-time basis: weekly salary times fifty-two weeks for hourly wage earners.

Next calculate a 25 percent benefits package value, even if you do not receive any benefits. Add these together and you have your personal earnings total. The low figure is the amount you were earning at the beginning of the record period, and the highest figure is the amount you were making at the end of the record period. Use the last six months as the period of record.

The next step is to add the personal earnings record and the market value together. Then divide that sum by two. On that quotient, calculate another 25 percent benefits package. Add this figure to the previous sum and you have a predetermined range from which to work out what jobs are appropriate for you, in what fields, for which employers.

To assess your personal market value you must have evaluated your financial needs, as well as your job satisfaction needs. No one makes the choice of which position to assume solely on the financial gain. It is not wise to do so. You need to figure the turndown point in salary amounts based on your financial responsibilities and needs. You have a picture of a realistic high if you do the research carefully and the computation correctly.

But you also must consider your own job satisfaction needs in addition to compensation. Beginning on the next page, there are evaluation charts to use to assist you in evaluating your position against salary and job satisfaction needs, as well as computing your own personal market value. There are a sample and blank form for your use.

◼ *COST OF LIVING INDEX*

An additional concept for research here would be the cost of living in the place where you plan to live. The American Chamber of Commerce Researchers Association in Washington, D.C., produces the *Inner-City Cost of Living Index,* which is updated quarterly. The information researched reflects the costs of housing, transportation, and various consumer items within one city and compares them with other cities using a predetermined national average or 100 percent city.

The city chamber of commerce must participate in the survey to be ranked this way. To determine whether a salary offer is good for the area, one must look at this index and compare. A salary of $35,000 looks great unless you must live in New York, Honolulu, or San Francisco. Then it is barely enough to survive.

JOB ACCEPTANCE CRITERIA

Job Satisfaction Value		*Compensation*	$_____
Rate on a scale of 1–10		Write in dollar amounts	
Meet Career Objective	_____	Salary	$_____
Room for Advancement	_____	90-Day Review	_____
Challenging Work	_____	Annual Salary	_____
Use Developed Skills	_____	Benefits	_____
People Environment	_____	Insurance	_____
Private Work Space	_____	Major Medical	_____
Geographic Preference	_____	Life Rider	_____
		Accident	_____
Management Style		ST Diability	_____
Authoritarian	_____	LT Disability	_____
Patriarchal	_____	Dental	_____
Participative	_____	Eye	_____
Laissez faire	_____	Pregnancy	_____
Product	_____	Individual	_____
Service	_____	Family	_____
Product and Service	_____	HMO	_____
Profit	_____	PPO	_____
Nonprofit	_____	Other	_____
Room for Creativity	_____	Vacation/Time Off	
Moving Expenses to Negotiate	$_____	Days Vacation	_____
Moving Furniture	_____	Holidays	_____
House-Hunting Trip	_____	Sick Leave	_____
Interviewing Expenses	_____	Personal Leave	_____
Lodging/Food Expenses	_____	Education Cap	_____
Spouse/Child Career/		Complete Degree	_____
School Placement	_____	Seminars,	
Other Potential Work Costs	$_____	Workshops,	
		Conventions	_____
Car/Travel Allowance	_____	Family Options	_____
Expense Accounts	_____	Other Benefits	_____
		Pensions	_____
		Bonuses	$_____
		Stock Options	_____
		Box Seats	_____
		Outplacement Costs	_____
		Indigenous Benefits	_____
		Other	_____

JOB ACCEPTANCE CRITERIA SAMPLE

Job Satisfaction Value		*Compensation*		$34,325
Rate on a scale of 1–10		Write in dollar amounts		
Meet Career Objective	10	Salary	$26,000	
Room for Advancement	8	90-Day Review	1,050	
Challenging Work	10	Annual Salary		27,050
Use Developed Skills	10	Benefits		7,275
People Environment	8	Insurance		3,375
Private Work Space	8	Major Medical	$ 1,200	

Geographic Preference San Jose, Calif.

Management Style		Life Rider	
Authoritarian		Accident	750
Patriarchal		ST Diability	750
Participative	10	LT Disability	
Laissez faire		Dental	125
Product	5	Eye	150
Service	5	Pregnancy	400
Product and Service	10	Individual	
Profit	10	Family	XX
Nonprofit	0	HMO	
Room for Creativity	10	PPO	XX
		Other	

Moving Expenses to Negotiate	$14,000	Vacation/Time Off	
Moving Furniture	$4,000	Days Vacation	10
House-Hunting Trip	2,000	Holidays	10
Interviewing Expenses	2,000	Sick Leave	5
Lodging/Food Expenses	2,000	Personal Leave	5

Spouse/Child Career/				
School Placement	4,000	Education Cap		$ 3,000
		Complete Degree	XX	
Other Potential Work Costs	$6,000	Seminars,		
		Workshops,		
		Conventions		
Car/Travel Allowance	$ .25/mile	Family Options		
Expense Accounts	Credit Card			

	Other Benefits		400
	Pensions		
	Bonuses	$ 400	
	Stock Options		
	Box Seats		

Outplacement Costs _____

Indigenous Benefits $ 500

Other _____

MARKET VALUE DETERMINATION

To determine personal market value in a career search, investigate and evaluate the market record at that time and add your personal earnings record.

	Low	High	Average
MARKET RECORD (consider the last six months to a year time frame)			
Ads	_____	_____	_____
Agencies (include graduate placement)	_____	_____	_____
Chambers of Commerce (where you live)	_____	_____	_____
U.S. Department of Labor	_____	_____	_____
Peer Interviews (about 5–6 interviews)	_____	_____	_____
Average Totals	_____	_____	_____
PERSONAL EARNINGS RECORD (consider last six months to a year time frame)			
Value of Jobs Held (figure at full time)	_____	_____	_____
Calculate 25% Benefits Package (even if you do not receive benefits)	_____	_____	_____
Personal Earnings Total (add)	_____	_____	_____
SUMMARY			
Market Record	_____	_____	_____
Personal Earnings Record	_____	_____	_____
Sum	_____	_____	_____
Divide Sum by Two	_____	_____	_____
Calculate an Additional 25% Benefit Package	_____	_____	_____
Add Last Two Numbers in Columns (determines total compensation potential)	_____	_____	_____
Assess Personal Market Range	Turndown Point _____		
	Realistic Potential High_____		

MARKET VALUE DETERMINATION SAMPLE

To determine personal market value in a career search, investigate and evaluate the market record at that time and add your personal earnings record.

	Low	High	Average
MARKET RECORD (consider the last six months to a year time frame)			
Ads	$22,000	$28,000	$25,000
Agencies (include graduate placement)	22,000	29,000	24,500
Chambers of Commerce (where you live)	20,000	30,000	25,000
U.S. Department of Labor	18,000	35,000	26,500
Peer Interviews (about 5–6 interviews)	22,000	26,000	25,000
Average Totals	$20,400	$29,600	$25,000

PERSONAL EARNINGS RECORD (consider last six months to a year time frame)	Low	High	Average
Value of Jobs Held (figure at full time)	$18,000	$20,000	$19,000
Calculate 25% Benefits Package (even if you do not receive benefits)	+ 4,500	+ 5,000	+ 4,750
Personal Earnings Total (add)	$22,500	$25,000	$23,750

SUMMARY	Low	High	Average
Market Record	$20,400	$29,600	$25,000
Personal Earnings Record	+22,500	+25,000	+23,750
Sum	$42,900	$54,600	$48,750
Divide Sum by Two	21,450	27,300	24,375
Calculate an Additional 25% Benefit Package	+ 5,363	+ 6,825	+ 6,094
Add Last Two Numbers in Columns (determines total compensation potential)	$26,813	$34,125	$30,469

Assess Personal Market Range   Turndown Point ____$27,000____

                                      Realistic Potential High____$34,125____

EXAMPLE: If $25,000 is the offer (or previously determined acceptable salary by the candidate), how does this salary compare with the cost of living indices in the three cities being compared?

City #1	95.1	×	$25,000	=	$23,775
City #2	127.2	×	$25,000	=	$31,800
City #3	112.5	×	$25,000	=	$28,125

Results: $25,000 is a good salary for City #1. ($1725+) You might buy a car!
$25,000 is a poor salary for City #2. ($6800−) You're going to live in your car.
$25,000 is below average for City #3 ($3125−) You're going to walk everywhere you go.

Using these concepts will prepare you to enter the searching phase of your campaign. Knowing who you are (résumé), where you are going (marketing plan), how skillful you are (skills portfolio and keyword stripe), where job satisfaction and commensurate compensation lie (job acceptance criteria), how much you are probably worth to the chosen market (market value determination), and what the cost of living is in the city of your choice (cost of living index), is needed for a successful marketing campaign.

■ *NEGOTIATION SKILLS*

Negotiation skills consist of self-knowledge (career goal or focus, personal market value with an identified turndown point), knowledge of the economy and its relationship to the field being investigated, and the theories of *Game Theory* as applied to salary negotiation, honesty, patience, and self-esteem. The negotiating candidate needs to understand thoroughly the factors involved in the negotiation, be aware of the monetary value of these factors, and have a personal decision value placed on each factor in order to plan a negotiating session.

The factors involved are the salary, the benefits package, and any other exchange of funds or items of value for accepting a position. Before real negotiations can begin, you must have a negotiation session where information is exchanged. The salary range, 90-day reviews, and any other items that pertain to compensation must be discussed.

■ *SALARY AND BENEFITS*

The benefits package needs to be clarified. Benefits usually are made up of three major categories: insurance, education, and vacation/time off. You need to understand the insurance benefits after reading the materials concerning insurance packages offered in the company. Insurance coverage can be handled by three, four, or five different insurance companies that may offer a variety of services within their packages. Read carefully so that you understand what the company is going to pay and what you are going to pay for which services. Then make sure your understanding is accurate and clarify what is not understood. Ask questions; do not assume anything about insurance packages.

Next, examine the education benefits. Ask about the philosophy behind the policy. How much education money is available for an employee to use for continuing education? What parameters are put on the accumulation of credit hours toward another degree, if any?

Many companies have an education cap. This cap usually applies to the amount of money a company will invest in continuing education for each employee. Every company has its own policies about who is eligible for the money, what kind of education or training is funded, and whose permission must be sought to begin educational ventures that you expect the company to fund.

Some companies will pay for employees to go to seminars, workshops, or conventions in their fields as long as the expenses of attending these events do not exceed the education cap for one year. What is the policy about this? Educational institutions often make education classes for family members available at a reduced rate. The employee negotiates this if it is needed or wanted. This policy usually applies only to educational and training facilities. It is important for you to know, so be diligent in pursuit of this information during the first negotiation session.

The best time for you to ask a company to consider assisting you with your accumulated debt for your current education is when these costs are in line with their policy on education caps for employees and before you are hired. Six months later it will be a dead subject. Now you have a state-of-the-art, recently earned degree, and it has value to companies. Very quickly you will need additional educational options to stay current in your field.

When would you consider this as an option? If you do not want to go back to school immediately upon going to work, this presents a good opportunity. If you want to expend your own funds for graduate courses and maximize the educational cap that first year to assist you with your accumulated education loan, this could be feasible.

You probably will not reach the education cap available to you by attending a master's degree program, so negotiating student loan payments with the available education cap funds becomes a plus for you. With this option the company continues to fund state-of-the-art education. The company negotiator probably explained something like this when you asked about its education policy. Quote it back when you are negotiating for something the negotiator may have never considered. For example, you may want the company to consider its education policy in light of your need to pay your student loan.

Vacation/time off policy also needs clarification. Exactly what are the rules about the standard vacation? Must the vacation be taken all at once? If you stretch vacation time out over the year, what are the rules? What holidays are celebrated by the company with time off? If you work overtime on a project is money awarded or can time off be a form of compensation? Religious holidays are allowed as days off if they are different than those the predominant culture celebrates. What is the policy on this issue? Is there a possibility of time being allotted for infrequent but important family celebrations like parents' silver or golden wedding anniversaries or family reunions? What are the rules about time away from your job as a compensation for your time on the job?

What is the philosophy behind sick-leave policies? Is the sick leave cumulative if not taken annually as allowed? Is there a reward for remaining healthy and not needing the time off for sickness? What about personal-leave days? To whom are these awarded? An employee does not have to give the manager a reason for asking for a personal day, only sufficient time to arrange for the employee's absence.

There was a national Family and Medical Leave Act passed in the early days of the Clinton administration. How does this business apply that law to its employees' needs for family care? Again, assume nothing because all companies have a variety of ways they comply with the laws and arrange for employee benefits regarding time off. They have negotiated with others according to company policy. You need to know all of that information before you can negotiate adequately for yourself.

The reimbursement policy for moving expenses needs to be understood before you contract for a moving company's services. Policies about moving expenses vary widely. Some companies and the federal government will not move you to the first position you take with them. However, they will pay for all moves you make, after your first position, that require you to move to continue working for them.

Some companies give you a lump sum, and it is up to you to get to the job site on time. Some have contracts with major movers and all you need to do is set the date and the moving company will arrive, pack your things, whisk them to your new address, and unload. Others expect you to move yourself and submit a voucher upon arrival. Know that moving companies will not move you unless you prepay. Be prepared for that expense up front and know that your reimbursement may take forty-five to sixty days because of a company's bookkeeping system.

In all cases you need to know what the rules are about reimbursing you for moving expenses. These include moving you and all your worldly goods, house-hunting trips with other family decision makers, and interviewing expenses, and they could include spouse or child career-or school-placement counseling, if this is needed. Have all the information clear in your head so you can plan for your second negotiation session with an informed approach.

Other benefits may include pensions, bonuses, stock options, availability of box seats for cultural events or sports activities, outplacement costs if needed, and other indigenous benefits. Pensions are available to all employees at different lengths of employment. What is the company's policy? Most will have a 401K plan or something similar, but you need to know the options and the rules.

Bonuses are awarded in a variety of ways. They could be attached to the entire company's performance, to a special project within the company, to a special department within the company, and so forth. Again, what are the policies?

Stock options are sometimes given in lieu of salary compensation. You can sell these yourself if you want the money, or you can keep them and reap the dividends if there are any. In both cases you will be taxed for these benefits. Being taxed is not necessarily a reason to refuse the benefit. Consider it in light of all the other benefits, your own personal financial portfolio, and your personal interests.

Indigenous benefits are available in some companies. They may include box seats at the major sports arenas and performing theaters as a matter of tax benefit to the company. Companies may then make these events available to some or all personnel. Again, what is the policy? Usually these seats are available to employees because of their position in the company. Often this means the seats are available to management, sales personnel, and executives only.

It may seem inappropriate to negotiate outplacement costs at the beginning of employment with a company, but it will be impossible to negotiate them at the time of severance. This is also governed by policy. If the company says it does not have a policy, then it may be time to consider one at, or by the time of, your second negotiation session.

Trailing-spouse benefits that have been negotiated with some companies include the following:

1. Philosophically, companies are willing to give whatever it takes to persuade the most valued candidate from its perspective, as well as its own employees, to relocate to key jobs in the company.
2. The squeaky wheel still gets the most attention in American corporate politics. Do not be obnoxious about this, but keep your name and your potential before the decision makers at all times.
3. Companies are willing to give cash awards to a trailing spouse who gives up a professional position. Amounts usually vary from $4,000 to $5,000. In a few cases spouse A is able to negotiate a quiet reimbursement of spouse B's full year of lost revenue.

EXAMPLE: Spouse A takes a new position and moves from San Diego, Calif., to San Jose, Calif. Spouse B had to quit a professional position to accompany spouse A to the new city. Spouse A negotiated three months' salary for spouse B for lost income, and $1,500 to help spouse B launch an entrepreneurial effort in San Jose.

Spouse A accepts a new job. Spouse B takes over parent's business 100 miles away from current home. Spouse A negotiated a telecommunications package and network interface (including a 56K telephone line and a network interface) that requires spouse A to be in the office one day a week and work the rest of the time from the home office.

Intel pays for four round-trip air tickets a year (business class to Europe; first class to Asia) for spouses who do not accompany their mates around the globe.

Sometimes the company will also employ the spouse of its new employee. Motorola employs thirteen spouses in China on a contractual basis.

(Source: Marshall Loeb, "You, Inc." in *FORTUNE* Magazine, April 15, 1996.)

Could you handle this level of negotiation? It is possible, but you must have good self-esteem, be greatly desired by the company decision makers, and able to demonstrate that it will be worth it for them to provide you with these benefits. Not a task for the faint of heart.

Some other indigenous benefits are those rooted in the nature or business of the company. If a company manufactures software, it may make older versions of software available to its employees free of charge. If a company is in the tax-preparation business, it may make tax preparation available to all employees who want that service at a reduced rate or no charge. The company may deliver a product or service that would also be useful to its employees. It may have a policy about making these products or services available at a reduced rate or at no charge to employees. If there is such a policy, what does it mean?

Then there are company policies about how employees are reimbursed for money spent doing company business; credit cards and voucher systems are two possibilities. How is money spent on entertaining clients or doing the general business of the company returned to the employee? What is the policy in this matter?

First Negotiation Session

You can see how valuable the first negotiation session is in clarifying policies, understanding limitations, and knowing the rules and options available for all benefits. Now you are ready to consider a plan to negotiate the benefits you want and judge how they might apply to your strategy of negotiating. Even though this requires you to think carefully, it is something a graduate looking for a first position can do.

Be careful, plan well, consider all options, evaluate options in terms of value to you, their value in the company, and their value in the marketplace.

Game Theory

John von Neumann, an Austrian mathematician and philosopher of the nineteenth century, developed *Game Theory*. He designed a system whereby the principles of mathematics are applied to other situations within or outside of mathematics to enable decision makers to arrive at the most beneficial resolution. His methods have been adapted in this chapter to assist you in negotiating the best possible deal available for a position.

Now you are ready to plan your second negotiation session. You have much more information than you had before the session started. Look at how *Game Theory* can be applied to your negotiation strategy. First, identify the factors that are important to you. These will include things like salary, tuition reimbursement, medical benefits, sales commissions, territory control, company future, pension plans, company car, and reasonable professional control of the position. No job will have all of these factors. Some of you will want to consider factors that do not appear here. It is crucial to identify the factors that are important to you and prioritize them.

Second, determine the actual monetary value for each factor identified.

1. Salary range.
2. Tuition reimbursement and associated education cap.

3. Medical benefits correlated with insurance costs.
4. Sales commission (couple rates with policy).
5. Territory control identified with procedures.
6. Company future compared with annual reports.
7. Pension plans.
8. Company car related to work assigned.
9. Control of profession based on your education, experience, and company practice.

Third, make a personal decision on a 100 percent scale about what value each of these factors has to you. What meaning does this individual factor have in relation to whether you want this job or another? How does this factor weigh in relation to all of the other things you have to consider upon accepting this position? Remember that you are looking for the best option among many good opportunities. See the next page for an option to consider and think about seriously for yourself.

On paper it looks like this process would take about two minutes. This is not true. The first item to be negotiated is salary, and it needs to be negotiated all the way down to the agreed salary. You need to give reasons for each counteroffer based on what was communicated about policy and salaries in the first negotiation session. If the salary cannot be agreed upon at this time both parties can agree to put it on hold until after the benefits package is negotiated.

The tuition reimbursement is next. Each time you want to counter the company's offer, you must give a rationale. Base this rationale on the philosophy stated by the original negotiator in the first session. It shows that you are applying the company's philosophy or rationale to this figure request that you want to negotiate.

Whenever you counter in any segment of the negotiation be sure you use the company's policies, procedures, and rationale for asking for the higher figure or a better condition. It will never be given to you just because you want it. There must be some justification for the figure negotiated. Help the company give you what you want by using its own procedures and policies to defend what your counteroffer suggests.

In this scenario the medical benefits were never in conflict. The vacation benefit was in conflict all the way to the last item of agreement. This means that the company really wants the candidate to come to work immediately. This could be because there is a special project on the line that would require the candidate's skills and experience.

The candidate must discover why the company is so insistent on no vacation; then it will be easier to negotiate effectively. Let the company know you are willing to compromise your requests when you understand what the company has in mind for you. You might have received some of this information in the first session if you had picked up on the need for your skills and how much the timing of your employment means to the company.

Some graduates feel insecure about negotiating and just want to take what is offered and begin working. At stake is your future career, in which monetary advances will be made in relation to your beginning salary in this career. Salaries are a matter of record and can be discovered by a determined employer.

You can learn these skills. Exercises to practice until you gain some confidence are to visit an outdoor market and negotiate a price different from the list price for the items. Go to a garage sale and never pay the list price; always negotiate a lower price. Go for a job interview in a situation where you do *not* really want the job and see how far you can go with your negotiation skills. You can always say no because the job does not pay enough, the company does not have an education cap, the medical benefits are really substandard, the distance you would have to travel was more than you had planned, or your opportunity for advancement was not clear.

Negotiation is both a set of skills and an art. The skills are self-knowledge (career goal or focus, personal market value, turndown point), knowledge of the economy in your chosen field, and *Game Theory* as it is applied to salary negotiation, honesty, patience, and self-esteem. The art embodies sensitivity, interpersonal communication, etiquette, and self-awareness. This is indeed a tall order, and only the brave of heart—you— will succeed.

SCENARIO

Accounting graduate with *magna cum laude* record, who held the office of president of the student council in her senior year, is looking for a job to begin a new career. She hopes to succeed in this new position, prepare for a CPA exam, get married, and have a family within the next five years of her life. She has made a decision now that she would like to be a career woman who also has a family.

Factors	Monetary Value	Personal Decision Value
Salary	$25,000–33,000	75 percent
Tuition Reimbursement	Entire cap $5,000	15 percent
Medical Benefits Package	Best of it	5 percent
Immediate Vacation	(Two weeks without pay: a break after school and before assuming the job.)	5 percent

PROCESS

Salary	Scale Point	×	Decision Value	=	Weight	Tuition	Scale	×	Decision Value	=	Weight
$33,000	10		0.75		7.5	$5,000	10		0.15		1.5
32,000	8		0.75		6.0	4,000	8		0.15		1.2
31,000	7		0.75		5.25	3,000	6		0.15		0.9
30,000	6		0.75		4.5	2,000	4		0.15		0.6
29,000	5		0.75		3.75	1,000	2		0.15		0.3
27,000	4		0.75		3.0						
26,000	2		0.75		1.5						
25,000	1		0.75		0.75						

Vacation	Scale Point	×	Decision Value	=	Weight	Medical Benefits	Scale Point	×	Decision Value	=	Weight
2 weeks	10		0.05		0.5	Best	10		0.05		0.5
1 week	5		0.05		0.25	Average	6		0.05		0.3
None	0		0.05		0	Poor	2		0.05		0.1

Applicant wants:	35,000,	$5,000 education cap,	best medical,	and 2 weeks off.	
Decision Value	7.5 +	1.5 +	0.5 +	0.5 =	10.0

NEGOTIATION SESSION #2

Company offers:	$29,000,	$2,500 education cap,	best medical,	and no vacation.	
Decision value	3.75 +	0.75 +	0.5 +	0 =	5.0

Applicant counters $35,000, $5,000 education cap,   best medical, and two weeks vacation.

Company counters	$31,000,	$4,000 education cap,	best medical,	and no vacation.	
Decision value	5.25 +	1.2 +	0.5 +	0 =	6.95

Applicant counters $32,000, $5,000 education cap,   best medical, and two weeks vacation.

Decision value	6.0 +	1.5 +	0.5 +	0.5 =	8.5

Company counters $32,000, $5,000 education cap,   best medical, and one week vacation.

Decision value	7.5 +	1.5 +	0.5 +	0.5 =	10.0
Decision value	6.0 +	1.5 +	0.5 +	0.25 =	8.25

Applicant agrees.

Chapter 6 has covered vital material relating to successfully landing the job of your dreams after you have located it. Knowing your own market value is critical to your self-knowledge and self-esteem. It is fun to begin learning negotiation skills if you do not already possess them. Practice in environments that are not so emotionally charged for you as job negotiation might be. *Game Theory* and its application make complicated issues seem more understandable and conflicts can be resolved more easily.

Chapter 6 Challenges

Technological

1. Name the skills needed in negotiation and demonstrate to what degree you think you have these skills with a chart, table, or graph. See whether you improve by the end of the campaign.
2. Chart salary records for given degrees from information obtained from ads, graduate-placement offices, placement agencies in your chosen field, and peer interviews.
3. Develop a campaign chart for the costs of living in five major cities where you might like to live. Which is the best choice for cost of living?
4. Chart the differences between negotiation sessions one and two as you understand them.
5. For the last six-month period track your personal earnings record and compare it against the market value of your degree and skills for the same period.

Traditional

1. How would you determine your market value in your chosen career field?
2. Explain to a colleague how placement agencies work. How successful are they? How do you know this? Did you research it or are you guessing? Who pays the agencies? How is the fee calculated? Do you pay anything?
3. Where is the record of your personal earnings over the last year? Transfer that information to page 63.
4. Complete the job acceptance criteria for yourself on page 61.
5. Develop questions to make sure you have uncovered all of a company's policies, procedures, and practices that pertain to your own negotiation information bank.
6. Design some creative requests you might make of a company in exchange for asking your spouse to leave a good job and accompany you 1,200 miles to your new job. Then negotiate it skillfully. You can do it. Just be careful and prepare well.

Vocabulary

Recheck the correct definitions for the terms listed and be prepared to demonstrate that you understand them in relation to your own job search.

benefits
candidates
chamber of commerce
company car
compensation
cost of living
credit cards
decision value
earning power
education
Family and Medical
   Leave Act
federal government

Game Theory
graduate placement
indigenous
market value
monetary value
negotiate
network interface
outplacement
pensions
performance
personal earnings
personal leave
placement agencies

religious holidays
relocation
resolution
salary
sick leave
stock options
trailing spouse
tuition reimbursement
turndown point
U.S. Department of
   Labor
wage earners

Chapter 7

CANDIDATE VISIBILITY

LEARNING OBJECTIVES

After you study this chapter, you should be able to

- Design and formulate a professional résumé for your career choice.
- Devise and project your résumé into a variety of technical forms: interactive disk, slide presentation, demonstration disk, ASCII text for Internet float, Web page, and so forth.
- Make available a variety of cover letter templates to use for interviewing purposes.
- Create a mini résumé or market letter.
- Develop an approach to the hidden market.
- Outline letter templates for inquiries to businesses and chambers of commerce.

- Lay out an acceptance letter and a withdrawal-from-consideration template.
- Generate a variety of professional networking letters for peer contacts and decision-maker contacts.
- Track your contacts using the database located in appendix I.
- Read about etiquette in business practices, discuss etiquette issues with those you recognize as practitioners of this art, and keep focused on the other person(s) to practice good business etiquette.

LEARNING PROCESSES / SKILLS

RÉSUMÉ CONTENT

Identification
Career Objective
Skills Profile
Education
Experience
Keyword Stripe

RÉSUMÉ FORMAT

One Page
ASCII Text
Demonstration Disk
Slide Show
Web Home Page
Video
Curriculum Vitae

LETTER TEMPLATES

Target
Broadcast
Peer/Decision-Maker Network
Market/Mini Résumé
Inquiry
Acceptance/Withdrawal
Professional Network

NETWORKING

Etiquette
Business Cards
Communication
Netiquette

■ RÉSUMÉ

As a candidate for a career position you cannot afford to be anonymous in the process. The more people who know you are looking for a good position in your chosen field, the more help you will receive. So the question becomes one of visibility. How visible are you and how visible is your résumé? These issues have been alluded to earlier in this text, but now the focus will be on them directly.

Visibility tools include your résumé, a variety of cover letters, some knowledge of the Internet, and the etiquette that reigns there as well as in business generally. Networking skills are explained and outlined in this chapter. This skill base often gets overlooked because people assume everyone knows how to do it. Networking is generally one of the things people do least competently in a search.

Your résumé must be impeccable in form, whatever form is used: one-page paper résumé, ASCII text résumé, demonstration disk résumé, slide-show interactive résumé, Web home page, video, and so on. The purpose of the résumé is to engage the reader, to arouse the reader's interest, and to invite the reader to absorb the information on the résumé in order to gain an interview.

As we have seen earlier, the résumé also "says more about you than the résumé says!" Misspelled words say volumes that your degree work cannot cover. Irregular columns and margins indicate that you cannot use certain software no matter what you claim to know.

English usage errors could eliminate you from a position. If you format a disk for interactive use, it must be usable in most technical environments where you send it, otherwise it looks like you cannot or did not format the résumé yourself. If you have spelling errors on your slide for an interactive slide show with résumé information, you will lose your audience at first try.

If your résumé is not clearly in ASCII text to float on the Internet, it makes no difference how it looks on your computer if it is filled with machine language plus your résumé information on the reader's computer screen.

No reader will continue to read résumés with obvious errors. It is an annoyance. Again, "the résumé says more about you than the résumé says!"

Format aside, the résumé should make clear to the reader where you are going (career objective), what skills you possess to go there (skills profile), your education credentials and certifications (education), and your work history that supports your skill base (experience). If you choose to use a keyword stripe, it will highlight the focus you want the reader to have before he or she looks at your résumé more carefully. Reread chapter 4 carefully if you have forgotten the skills of producing a good résumé.

■ *LETTERS*

Cover Letters

Cover letters have different purposes. They are used to explain to a reader why you want your résumé to be considered. They usually are divided among target, broadcast, peer network, and decision-maker network letters, which basically describe each one's function. The cover letter that answers an ad is referred to as a target letter. Its function is to

- Identify how you know about the job.
- Know what qualifications you have to meet the job's requirements.
- Meet the qualifications for the position you know is open.

Use traditional block format for your return address and date, and the company's representative and address. Include a proper greeting and close your three paragraphs with a business closing. Allow four line spaces for a signature above your typed name.

As with most business letters, you will do well to follow a simple format for the letters.

- The first paragraph explains how you know the person you are addressing.
- The second paragraph tells the reader what you want.
- The third paragraph explains what help you intend to be to the business concerning the matter at hand.

(See appendix G for addressing envelopes.)

Identify how you know about the job. For example, you read it in the paper, a friend notified you of the opening, or you read it on the bulletin board in the company's office. The second paragraph gets more attention if you arrange it in two columns. Column A can be called requirements; list them as the company listed them in the ad. Do not put down a requirement that you do not meet. Column B can be titled qualifications; list how you feel you are qualified for the position.

EXAMPLE: Requirements   Qualifications

               B.S. degree   B.S. (Marketing) University of Kansas
                                                     magna cum laude

               2 years management experience   Three years managing a fast-food operation
                                                     while attending college.

               Computer skills   WordPerfect 5.0, Microsoft Word 6.0, Access
                                                     2.3, Excel 3.5, PowerPoint 5.4. Laboratory
                                                     work during degree studies for three years.

Paragraph three explains what you intend to do:

- First, enclose a résumé that outlines your interest and preparation for this position.
- Second, tell them you will call them on a specific date to arrange for an interview to discuss the details of the open position.
- Third, tell them you are pleased to discover this open position and are looking forward to discussing the requirements for the job in greater detail.
- End the letter with an appropriate close: Yours truly, Sincerely yours.
- Sign the letter.
- Allow four line spaces for your signature above your typed name.

The purpose of the broadcast letter is just that. It is an announcement that you are ready to move to a new city, a new field, or both. The broadcast letter is usually mailed to personnel officers in about thirty to forty companies in the area where you hope to live. In each letter you do as suggested earlier.

- Paragraph one explains how you know the company or the person to whom you are writing.
- Paragraph two explains why you want to talk with this individual.
- Paragraph three explains what you are going to do.

A good sentence to include in the second paragraph is the following: "I do not expect you to have a position for me or to know where one exists." This assures the reader that you are indeed looking for information in a new field or a career field in a new city. Do not use any bait-and-switch tactics. It will ruin your reputation and your chances of succeeding. Identify more clearly in paragraph two what you alluded to in paragraph one about the topics you want to discuss with the personnel director. Paragraph three identifies when you will be available in the new city to call and set up a meeting. As with the target letter, you include a copy of your résumé for the reader to consider. You should close every letter with a cordial ending to your inquiry.

The network letters are at two different levels. One is a peer network letter, which asks the reader for some time to discuss the field and the way things really are and possibly to assess what a given candidate's chances are of finding employment in the field. As in the other two letters, you need to explain in paragraph one how the reader is known and what you wish to discuss in your potential meeting.

The second paragraph also contains the sentence introduced in the broadcast letter: "I do not expect you to have a job for me or to know where one exists." The third paragraph explains that you are enclosing a résumé, when you will call to set up a meeting at the reader's convenience, and your thoughts and feelings about having your questions answered honestly by someone in the field. Close as indicated earlier.

The second network letter is that directed to the decision maker. Its purpose is to assist you to understand how decision makers think about the field. Their vision will be long range. Usually they arc aware of the competition. They look for talent appropriate to meet the future needs of the company. They are also cognizant of the industry's changing face.

But the format of the letter remains the same. Paragraph one identifies how you know this person. In the decision-maker network letter case, you should know the individual personally or have a reference from a mutual acquaintance. Also state why you want to talk with this person. Follow the directives given earlier for the second paragraph. Elaborate more about what you want to discuss and assure the person that you do not expect him or her to locate a job for you. Close your letter with paragraph three similar to the one in the peer network letter.

After reading all of this about not telling decision makers you are looking for a job, you may feel that this is a useless exercise. The purpose of these letters is to begin building a network in your chosen field. You have been hidden in your college for several years and are not known in the field of your choice. You need to get out and about for information, clues to your interviewing style, knowledge about how leaders see the future, and your place in it. This is all valuable information.

This method provides access to the so-called hidden market described in many books. It is not hidden, but this is the best way to break into the market and have responsible people know about you. If there is a job available in any place you go for a networking call, you can rest assured the job will be offered if they like what they see in you. This happens often. It depends on how the interviewer is or is not impressed with you, your credentials, and your style. No job is ever offered where there is no opening.

This networking process provides access to 68 percent of the job market. This is less than the Department of Labor's figure of 80 percent in 1990. You cannot afford to ignore it or the proper etiquette that will get you an interview. Some people think that cold calling is appropriate in job searching.

Cold calling is an impolite sales technique of calling on people you hope will give you an order even though you arrive unannounced and with no appointment to meet with the intended buyer or representative. This procedure is rude, because it seems to presume you think the person has nothing to do and so will be available just because you arrive. They may treat you courteously but quickly. You will have made a poor impression. Prepare your tactics better so that you give people advance notice that you would like to talk with them. What you have in common with them is the career field.

Marketing Letter/Mini Résumé

The marketing letter is a specially designed letter to meet the business policy that some companies have used to save their executives from being bothered with people who indiscriminately target top decision makers in their job search campaigns. There may come a time when you need to speak to the president of a company or the executive vice president of a branch of a company, but this will be toward the end of your campaign. This letter is used to get in to see an executive when you are absolutely sure you want a job with a specific company and have been unable to get a referral into the executive suite.

A marketing letter looks and reads differently than all the other letters in this chapter. It is not a cover letter. Some texts refer to it as a mini résumé. This letter begins with the best statement you can make about your top achievement.

EXAMPLE: "Recently I read your article, 'The Political Ramifications of the Flat Tax on Young People Entering Their Career Fields.' This was in *FORTUNE* Magazine in late December. I have been troubled by other comparisons people are making, since my senior project dealt with the flat tax and the 21st century. We seem to see eye to eye about some of these issues, and I would like to talk with you about them."

You might also list two or three other accomplishments about which you are particularly proud and include them in a shortened paragraph style.

EXAMPLE "Some other accomplishments I have achieved include

Earning a B.S. in three years with a cumulative GPA of 3.8 while working as a manager for a computer business during my last two years at school.

Designing a new accounting system for the business that has been accepted by the owner. I have been hired to install and implement the new system, which I anticipate will take me until graduation in three months.

Creating a database system that will assist my alma mater with its annual registration activities, reducing the time it takes the collegian to register by one-third to one-half the time it took in previous semesters."

Then close with an appropriate paragraph identifying your interest in meeting with this person and your enthusiasm for the individual's ideas as you understand them. Express a desire to have an opportunity to talk with this author. As you can see, this letter is different from the previous four letters.

Inquiry Letters

When doing research for a job search campaign you need information. Once you have identified companies where you think you could make a contribution and cities where you would like to live, you need to get information to support your decision. Letters that request such information are called inquiry letters and are sent to company marketing staffs and chambers of commerce executive directors. You want common information, so formulating your own form letters for these two functions will work effectively and save you time.

The inquiry letter to the chamber of commerce is another three-paragraph letter. In the first paragraph you identify why you are interested in the city and a little bit about what you expect to find in the city or were attracted to by advertising about its assets. Your requests are basically what you want a city to provide for you: city parks, concerts, theaters, sports arenas, newspapers, good transportation, good schools for the levels of your family's interests, medical support if needed, costs of buying or renting a home, cost of living, taxes and their uses, condition of the city with regard to safety, and more. You are limited only by what you want to know the city provides for you and your family after your nine-to-five job is finished. Remember that you can also get information from chambers' toll-free numbers, if you do not have time to wait for mail response.

The company inquiry letter is addressed to the marketing director (or some similar title). These are the people who have the information you want. You would like to have them send you copies of the annual report for the current year, a 10K report, if one exists, brochures about your professional

Avoid asking for a job or job leads in this letter because it is inappropriate. You do not know the company well enough to know whether you want a job with it. You appear overly anxious.

interests, which were identified in paragraph one, and identified addresses of business locations in the United States or elsewhere.

This letter is a three-paragraph business letter.

- Paragraph one explains how you became interested in the company, with specific details about your particular interest.
- Paragraph two is the request for four items: the annual report, the 10K report, if there is one, brochures about your interests, and a list of company addresses close to where you hope to live.
- Paragraph three is a basic business thank-you.

Format these letters and send them each time you want initial information about a company or a city of interest to you.

Accepting a Position

After you have negotiated the best deal for yourself and have verbally given the company your word that you will be the new employee, then sit down and formalize your job acceptance with an acceptance letter. This is sometimes called a memorandum of record. Although there are very few contracts good lawyers cannot figure out how to break, this memorandum of record has the force of being a legally binding document.

Therefore, be careful how you word your acceptance letter. It should contain the regular business letter format. In the first paragraph communicate how pleased you are to accept the position and name your new title. Assure your employer that this is exactly what you had hoped to find when you began your search and are happy to have found it.

Next, list the things you agreed to in the negotiations sessions as you remember them:

1. Time, day, and date you will appear for the new job.
2. Salary amount and date of first salary review.
3. Selection of insurance package, having returned whatever forms you needed to complete and possibly taking a physical examination.
4. Vacation time and how it will be taken by you, with whose approval.
   Any other holidays or religious observance days negotiated should be named and listed here in your letter.
5. Sick-leave and personal-leave policies as you understand them.
6. Education programs where you are to be registered over the coming year. Name the colleges, seminars, or conventions that were negotiated.
7. When and how you have prepared your records for those items to be reimbursed by the company upon presentation of the vouchers.
8. Appreciation for any trailing-spouse arrangements you have negotiated, such as career counseling, substitute pay for several months while your spouse looks for appropriate work in the new place, and so forth.

The next paragraph asks that you be notified if there is something you have misunderstood about the negotiation or if there is anything you have neglected to address. You want to be notified of these omissions, if there are any. Set the date for notification a few days before you will leave for the new city. Indicate that you will accept this memorandum of record as correct and in force if you have not heard from the company by a certain date. Tell your contact that you will call him or her when you arrive in the new city. The last paragraph is another expression of your pleasure at having found such a great position with the company. Thank the company for its consideration for your spouse, who is also a professional worker. Close with an expression of gratitude for all the courtesies that were extended to you over the period of interviewing before you were offered and accepted this new position.

End with your usual close and signature. Send courtesy copies of this letter to all who were a part of the final negotiation sessions. Identify who is receiving these courtesy copies at the foot of the letter.

EXAMPLE: cc: Jane Spriner, Vice President
Joe Falcon, District Manager
Edgar Nelson, Manager

Withdrawing Your Name

After you have accepted a new position, are on the job, and all points negotiated are in place, you need to have your name withdrawn from consideration by other companies with whom you were negotiating positions.

You write a three-paragraph business letter in which you express your regret (in the first paragraph) at withdrawing your name from the competition for (name the position), as of a certain date.

In the second paragraph explain that you have taken a position with (name the firm) and have discontinued competition for the job opening. Give a professional reason for having your name withdrawn at this time:

- Salary was too low for the responsibilities expected of you.
- Distance to the job was more extensive than you had anticipated.
- No real promotion possibilities or advancement in the company seemed possible for the next two or three years.

Whatever reason you give, be sure that at some point along the interviewing and negotiation sessions you have already expressed some reservations about the issue used here. Your rationale should not come as a surprise to the reader.

The third paragraph is a pleasant closing to this professional encounter with what you consider to be a good company. Leave the door open for future possibilities of working with it. Express your gratitude for the gracious treatment you received during the interviewing process. Close in your usual manner.

Professional Network Letter

Professional network letters are written to

- Peers
- Association members
- Support group members
- Any individuals you feel gave you great support
- People who shared important leads
- Persons who gave you a gracious hearing of your goals and objectives
- Others with good advice and counsel
- Those you want to retain in your network of professional contacts

Invite them to lunch or an association meeting you could both attend, express your gratitude for their help, and assure them that you will support them if and when they may need similar assistance. This is a basic three-paragraph business letter, written to a peer in your career field with whom you want to continue a professional relationship. This is a personal letter, not a form letter.

■ *ETIQUETTE*

Etiquette can be learned if you have none. Its basic premise is making the other person comfortable in your presence. Consider the other person's feelings and interests. Be conscious of time values. Speak respectfully. Ask politely for what you need. Be mindful of the person's time and potential to assist you realistically.

Most etiquette is learned at home where children's behavior is monitored and shaped. Coaches, who demand certain standards when the team leaves the locker room to go to the field or when it travels to another city for the contest, often take on this role of etiquette advisor. Teachers who take students on field trips and inform them of the proper behavior they expect are in this role.

Netiquette in cyberspace requires participants to consider the following:

Remember that you are writing to real people.

Be as courteous as if you were talking face to face.

Always check for usage errors before you send something over the Internet.

Never insult or demean another person's use of the 'Net.

Using capital letters is the equivalent of shouting on the Internet and unappreciated by the receivers.

Be brief and to the point, as you would be on the phone or in a business letter.

New graduates use a one-page résumé and one-page cover letters.

No cute stuff. Emoticons = emotions + icons. Do not use emoticons on anything associated with your professional search.

Avoid common anagrams in your search process; it is unprofessional.

In addition, today there is proper etiquette to be observed on the Internet. It is called "netiquette." Netiquette = network + etiquette. The term *netiquette* means a friendly user. Anything where people are involved demands a certain etiquette to lubricate smooth, human, verbal interchanges. Cyberspace is no different.

Business etiquette requires you to know how to meet strangers graciously. You can master the art of arranging meetings of strangers you hope will have some reason to continue a relationship. Know how to make introductions properly. Learn how to deal with waiters, wine stewards, table captains, bell boys, and anyone who does you a personal service.

These are all explained in various etiquette books. One of the best is by Letitia Baldridge, who was Jackie Kennedy's chief of protocol at the White House during Jack Kennedy's presidency. This book and others like it are revised often to keep current with business practice.

You can find these books in your local library. Study and be sensitive to others' feelings in professional settings and business meetings. Etiquette will gain you a great reputation, and you will become more confident in yourself as you concentrate on making others feel comfortable. You tend to forget your own insecurities, which is just another plus for the courteous professional.

◼ *NETWORK SKILLS*

Network skills will put you in a good place throughout your professional life. Most people do not make good use of networking opportunities, which are available all the time and everywhere. Anytime you meet a stranger in your campaign activities, be sure you take the time to introduce yourself carefully. Use your first name several times before you bring your family name into the conversation. Listen carefully when people tell you names by which they are known. Use them while talking with people and make a sincere effort to remember the family names that go with them.

If you have forgotten someone's name in a social or business setting, admit it and ask the person for a reintroduction. If you listen carefully you will soon have a reputation for remembering people's names. Individuals like to be remembered, so it is a skill well worth cultivating. Everyone can do it. All it takes is a certain sensitivity and patience.

Business cards are becoming a nuisance because they proliferate so. If you receive one, make a note to yourself later about why you want to remember this person. Do not give your business card to people indiscriminately. Have one ready for people who ask for your card but do not foist one on those who have no interest or intent of using the card to advantage.

When you are in a job search campaign it is important that everyone you meet knows what you are doing. You will be surprised at how many people respond favorably to the information and could make it possible for you to meet the person who will offer you the job of your dreams. The opportunities to network are only limited by your shyness and inability to converse with people. Get over shyness. This timidity is not a virtue and will stand in your way of achieving your goals.

Chapter 7 is replete with information that will make you a successful candidate for the job of your dreams. There is no magic, only hard work. "The devil is in the details" is an old saying, but it applies here. The more you pay attention to details, the better impression you will make and the sooner you will have a variety of options to consider.

Design and develop the most representative résumé that you can for your campaign: a one-page paper résumé, a demonstration disk résumé, a Web page on the Internet, an ASCII text file to float on the Internet, an interactive résumé, an interactive slide-show presentation of your creden-

Think about the following mantra for your continuous sales pitch, whether you are planning your day's agenda, setting meetings in your calendar, reviewing your notes before meeting a new person, coming back for second and third interviews, or negotiating the best deal for yourself.

"I am a college graduate.

I am different from others in this class because . . .

I hope to distinguish myself from the others with whom I may work by . . ."

tials, a video, and more alternatives are out there. Select the one that represents you and your readiness for the career market of your choice.

Create the most effective marketing plan you can design. Know how you are going to use your résumé effectively in your campaign. Have practice sessions with friends and relatives about interviewing techniques. Prepare for each interview by researching the company completely and being prepared to ask some hard questions about why you should bring your good name and your qualifications to the organization.

Interview skills improve with exercise. The more you interview the better you will be at it. Interviewers comment when they have met with a really successful interviewee. Sometimes they are amazed by the wide differences among interviewees.

Know what you are worth. This narrows the focus of your marketing campaign and keeps you from running into closed doors and inappropriate opportunities. You will not have your hopes so high that you will be crushed by the realities of what companies are willing to pay you for your services, education, experience, and skill level. You will be well informed and accurately aware of the real options for you. Realism wins.

Understand how complex it is to negotiate your own benefits and compensation package. The important part of your focus is to be able to negotiate for yourself fairly and squarely. You know what you are worth. You can use *Game Theory* to come up with what is reasonable. You will be respected by those companies with whom you negotiate because it is a skill they admire and respect. Cultivate it.

Being visible is the best way to have a successful campaign. Your résumé, letters, phone calls, interviews, chance meetings with people, networking, and basic etiquette are all one package that people observe going through the motions of a professional career search. You will make a favorable impression. Keep your wits about you. Practice patience and sensitivity when you are with others. Be visible and professional. It will reward you in the end.

Segment 2 covers a lot of material and challenges you to develop many skills. All of these skills will help you achieve your goal, the best job possible in your field. Readiness for the market will give you confidence that you can succeed. Promoting yourself in all the right places will help you achieve your goals. There is no such thing as one special job, and no other could accomplish it. Knowing your market value is another way of building your own confidence so that you will not take a job beneath your abilities or your worth in the marketplace. Being visible everywhere and all the time is now possible because of technology. Take advantage of it.

Chapter 7 Challenges

Technological

1. Check the templates on the disk that came with this book for format and usability. Design some of your own for those that are not to your liking or not adequately spaced for your prose.
2. Design a mini résumé for yourself and put it on the disk for safekeeping.
3. Study the qualifications for an acceptance letter and list them on your disk so that you remember them when you write your acceptance letter.
4. Do the same for a withdrawal letter. Copy to the disk for practice form.
5. Formulate a professional network letter for those who have been helpful to you. Save it on your disk for reference.

Traditional

1. Design a checking system for yourself that will alert you to misspelling and English usage errors; find people who are willing to proofread your creations.
2. Distinguish among the four cover letters for purpose, content, market, and goal in the marketplace and in your campaign plans.
3. Describe the hidden market. How would you try to enter this hidden market?
4. What is cold calling? Why is it deemed insulting by most decision makers?
5. Distinguish the mini résumé from your cover letters.
6. Draw topical differences between the two inquiry letters. How would you use them?
7. Do you think etiquette is old fashioned? Why? What word or phrase could be used in its place?
8. Why do you think collegians overlook networking skills?
9. How would you maximize the use of business cards, yours and others?
10. What are three etiquette questions and/or three attitudes you think college interviewees violate routinely? Construct a strategy to amend or change behavior in these areas. Share with your classmates and see whether they can learn from you and you from them.

Vocabulary

Differentiate between and among the eight different letter styles described in this chapter. Distinguish between a memorandum of record and a legal contract for employment. Describe and give examples of the seven different ways you can present your résumé information using as many words as are appropriate from the list.

accomplishments
anagrams
annual report
business cards
calendar
campaign
candidate
career position
chambers of commerce
cold calling
computer screen
cover letters
emoticons
etiquette

Game Theory
hidden market
Internet
interviews
leads
letters
   acceptance
   broadcast
   decision-maker network
   inquiry
   peer network
   professional network
   target
   withdraw name

market value
memorandum of record
netiquette
requirements
résumé
   ASCII text
   demonstration disk
   interactive
   one page
   slide show
   video
   Web page
visibility
10K report

Segment 3
MARKETING STRATEGY

In professional marketing vocabulary the four Ps are the core combination of information available, or the marketing mix. These include *product, promotion, price,* and *place,* with significant definitions for these four terms. The first analogy to use with a job search campaign is product. This is an accumulation of your education, experience, skill base, talent, and personal characteristics. You have focused these qualities on your résumé for a reader to consider.

Promotion implies personal selling and extensive advertising in your job search activities. You have developed tools for this in segment 2. They include your résumé, interviewing process and techniques, and the many places you will send your résumé in its varying formats.

The third marketing term translated into a job search campaign is price. In segment 2 you calculated a reasonable salary range to consider as an exchange for your services, education, and experience. This market value is not written in stone but gives a realistic guide for what you may be worth financially in the career marketplace.

Place refers to distribution in marketing terms. An analogy can be drawn here between distribution of goods and services in the traditional sense to the distribution of your résumé. The variety of levels of interviews you arrange, the twenty-four-hour visibility you make possible through technology, and your own good planning are but some of the ways you distribute information. You notify decision makers that you are prepared to accept a formal professional position in your career field.

Segment 3 is about strategy, which is the method and rationale whereby you establish direction in your marketing efforts. Some might say that they are in reverse order. You do not set a plan in motion until you have determined the direction you are going. In traditional marketing, that makes sense.

However, the time factors in a career search usually require the searcher to begin with the identifiable characteristics of a campaign: the résumé, the interviewing goals and process, the promotional effort, and the determination of the potential salary range expected. In many cases a strategy is never considered. The goal is to get a job only. You, however, are looking for the best options possible in your chosen career field, so you need to consider carefully a strategy into which your campaign plans fit and against which you can measure achievement.

Consider the distinctions between strategy and planning. Chapters 8, 9, and 10 will look seriously at your marketing aims, internal factors affecting those aims, and external factors affecting the achievement of market aims. Chapter 8 describes the time it takes to develop a résumé, the methods to use for market analysis in your career field, a way to identify a career focus that is clear to you, a marketing plan design that will assist you to achieve your goals, and considerations of budget matters regarding the expense of running a professional career search campaign.

Chapter 9 examines your personal or internal factors that might get in the way or be beneficial to goal achievement. These include a look at your disposition or attitude and ways to capitalize on your personality or individuality without appearing obnoxious and arrogant.

How does your newly accumulated knowledge affect your search: where you go, whom you see, why you choose the tools you do? Your degree has value. Do you know what that value is? Your experience and familiarity with the professional jargon, complex connections, and synthesis of pertinent information, theory, and practice are interwoven with your new skills. Your skills are many, hopefully focused to advantage on your résumé, and a sign to all who might be interested in the fact that you have some developed expertise. Chapter 9 enables you to look at these important facts that are all in your control.

Chapter 10 considers the external factors that will affect the achievement of your goals. Some of these factors are within your control and others are not, but all will affect your final success. The first consideration is given to those data known to you but that are very complex and mainly out of your control. These include the economy, the environment in which the career is focused, the society in which you live, the technology that grows exponentially in content, complexity, and variety, and the politics and law practices that govern industries and business policies.

You can know something about company policies and culture by doing adequate research with business profiles, interviewing, and market assessment. You may not be able to affect these topics, but you can know about them. You can also get a realistic picture of the competition facing you in a given field. You cannot change the competition's challenge to you, but you can alter your responses to those challenges in order to meet your goals more quickly and accurately.

Chapter 10 also accounts for immediate circumstances that are in your control. These include level of, purpose of, preparation for, research about, and date and time of interviews. Which job leads do you follow and to what extent are they in your hands? Communication skills, which are always subject to analysis and assessment, should continue to improve or you may lose them.

Decision making is in the control of the searcher. Only you can determine the extent to which you will accept someone's advice, negotiate for an open position, compare job offers, set limits to your pursuit, and decide which tactics are best for you. Discipline your approach to the market and determine which resources will produce the best options for you. You are in the cockpit. It is your journey.

Segment 3 concentrates on thinking about your goals, designing options you will use, evaluating the effectiveness of your choices, and basically understanding what you can and cannot control in relation to your job search. This segment is more about thinking than doing. Read carefully and tread lightly.

Chapter 8

MARKET AIMS

LEARNING OBJECTIVES _____

After you study this chapter, you should be able to

- Outline your market goals/aims.
- Print your most powerful résumé.
- Research and do market analysis in your own career field.
- Determine a long-term career focus, as well as your short-term career objective.
- Design and form an integral whole of your skills and the market needs in your chosen field.
- Formulate a complete marketing plan called a marketing strategy.

- Determine the budget limits of your marketing strategy.
- Research with InfoTrac and ProQuest to determine the best and most effective way to meet the marketplace.
- Use charts to visually measure how accurately your plan is working for you to attain your goals.
- Know the four Ps of marketing theory and be able to apply them to your own marketing strategy to attain your personal career goals.

LEARNING PROCESSES / SKILLS

RÉSUMÉ

Circulate in Professional Circles
Several Forms of Résumé
Conversational Tool

MARKET ANALYSIS

Research
Career Focus
Marketing Plan
Budget

CAREER ATTITUDE

Strategic Thinking
Contemporary Issues

Education Accent
Take Charge

MONEY ATTITUDE

Budget Carefully
Takes Money to Make Money
Dress Professionally

CAREER MARKETING

Place
Price
Promotion
Skills as Product

Do not turn the search over to someone else you deem could do a better job. No one can do a better job than you. There are advice and counsel available. Good and knowledgeable people to assist you. Friends and relatives to support you. But only you can search and find the best possible position.

To achieve your market goals you must prepare with care and caution, research with a sharp sense of inquiry, develop tools of significance, design strategies that will work effectively for you, and be watchful of your expenses. As a job searcher in highly competitive markets, you need to take charge of your search. You will be taking the job—not someone else.

■ RÉSUMÉ

The evolution of your résumé will come slowly and be changed somewhat as you seek advice about what might be the best way to present yourself in your career market. Once you have determined that you have the best résumé possible for you, then you need to design the formats in which you want the résumé to appear and the professional circles in which you want it to circulate. The content remains the same, while the format may change (see chapter 4).

Where you send your résumé, the format you choose, whom you are trying to impress with your résumé, what you hope to accomplish with your résumé, and why you are sending the résumé in this particular format are questions that only you can answer.

■ *MARKET ANALYSIS*

If you are aware of the times in which you live, you may recognize the help you need. There are analytical business journals in your field and in the general field of business published daily, weekly, monthly, quarterly, and annually. They are available to you in libraries and on the Internet. It costs little to download the information for later analysis.

Libraries have multiple services that make research possible and accurate. They include

- Abstracts
- Program presentations
- Government briefs
- Academic condensations
- Professional synopses
- Scholarly monographs
- Other ways to analyze the market, a specific industry, or a career field

You cannot afford to be unaware of the environment you are choosing to enter as a professional practitioner in the field.

Compare your preparation and background against what is happening in the market. This assessment and insight will help give direction to your search. Knowledge of the marketplace enables you to design an effective plan for working productively in that marketplace to achieve your goal.

■ *CAREER FOCUS*

Your career focus is broader than your career objective statement on your résumé. This is up to you, however. Some dream of where they will be ten or fifteen years down the line. Others just want to get the next job and successfully begin to use their education, experience, skill, and talents. Your career focus is personal and subject to change.

Some believe that life is what happens to you while you are preparing for something else. This may or may not be true, but it is an insight worth considering.

Where were you before entering college? Did you see yourself as needing an advanced degree, or did a sudden job loss help you determine you needed more education to succeed in the marketplace? We all have our motivating forces. What is important is understanding and making them a part of our decision-making processes with regard to career.

Listen to and reflect on the lyrics of "Beautiful Boy" by John Lennon, written to express his love and to give advice to his only child.

■ *MARKETING PLAN*

Design a career strategy that is a broad-based effort to determine a worldview about your career and the methods you will use to achieve your worldview. Your first steps were going to college, determining your major, successfully completing the rigorous curriculum designed for your major, and now graduating.

Next, maximize the benefits of your newly acquired education to gain the best job possible. This means you must

- Identify an immediate career objective.
- Understand how much support you have for reaching that career goal.
- Design a résumé that will impress the readers in content and format.
- Arrange for interviews with a wide variety of people.
- Know who can help you achieve your goal.
- Assess people's advice.
- Evaluate the leads people give you.
- Determine which leads to follow to achieve your goal.

In one or many of these interviews you will be offered positions to consider. This evolves to other considerations. Which offers are the best options for you at this time? Are you knowledgeable and savvy enough to negotiate for yourself effectively and confidently? Making decisions is a large part of this strategy because you are beginning your career. This position is the one you will step from to gain better employment or reject if you have not been careful in your selection process.

After you are started on your career path, you will always be looking for ways to improve yourself professionally, new options in which to use your existing skills, better opportunities in your field as they open and you become aware of them. Where will the economy lead the country, the world, the industry you are serving, or the business where you work? The future is uncertain. Not looking at it or preparing for its eventualities adds to the uncertainties. Segment 4 will give you some ideas to consider.

■ *BUDGETS*

It is expensive to conduct a job search campaign. You need to analyze how much money you can afford to spend on your job search. Be careful not to spend money for other people to do your work for you. You need to spend your money to have the best-looking résumé you can produce, to take significant people you want to interview to lunch for discussion and to "pick their brains," to travel for interviewing, to pay for résumé services, professional advising, typing or word processing fees (if needed), and Internet service.

HOW MUCH SHOULD YOU CONSIDER? (1996–1997 FIGURES)

Item	Description	Statistical Average	Current Costs
Résumé Preparation	Counseling with professional adviser	$80–150/hour	_____
	Typesetting résumé	80–100/page	_____
	Word processing résumé	25–35/page	_____
	Printing résumé	45–75/100 copies	_____
Cover Letters	Stationery/envelopes	$125–150/ream	_____
	Typing letters/envelopes	4–6/letter	_____
	Postage	First class	_____
Telephone	Long-distance calls	As needed	_____
	Local calls/pay phones	As needed	_____
Transportation	Air travel	As needed	_____
	Ground travel (taxi, bus, gas, parking fees, tolls, etc.)	As needed	_____
Food and Lodging	Restaurant expenses	As needed	_____
	Hotel/motel expenses	As needed	_____
Other	Newspapers/journals	As needed	_____
	Clothing	As needed	_____
	Meetings, courses, seminars	As needed	_____
Internet	Newspaper article	Free–$20	
	Patent search	$20–100	
	Scholarly journal article	$20–100	
	Recent statute	Free–$20	
	Text of legal opinion	Free–$20	
	Trademark search	$20–100	
	Publicly owned company background	$20–100	
	Privately owned company background	$20–300	
	Key topics overview to date	$20–300	
	Industry overview	$20–300	

There are several things to consider when providing a budget for job searching. You may not need résumé preparation if you still have this book. Advice would be helpful if you are changing fields or having a midlife crisis about your work. Printing costs vary widely, so shop for the best price. Use a laser printer if you are doing the work yourself. Always have the blackest ink on the whitest paper for the one-page résumé. Use something less sharply contrasted for the ASCII text résumé.

Stationery and envelopes should match and will if you purchase them at the same time. You will need a ream of paper and 250 matching envelopes. Take these papers and envelopes to the printer or whoever is going to do your printing and you will save a bundle. Sometimes high-school students will be willing to do the word processing or typing for you at reduced rates. Ask for samples of their work before you hire them.

Check the Internal Revenue Service (IRS) rules about job searching. They clearly say what can be deducted on your tax return. Receipts are always needed, as with any IRS expenditure you may have to justify later. Keep all receipts connected with your job search: telephone bills, airline tickets, taxi and bus fares, parking fees, toll charges, gas receipts, mileage records per day, restaurant accounts, hotel/motel charges, newspaper and journal costs, and any seminar, meetings, counseling sessions, or courses you take to become a better interviewer. If you have any out-of-pocket expenses not already listed, keep a journal account of these expenditures also. Use the current figures of the economy at the time you are doing your search.

The evolution of your résumé, a concise and accurate analysis of the job description in your chosen industry or field, a career focus that satisfies you, a marketing strategy that will work effectively for you, and a clear and realistic budget are all necessary in completing a successful campaign. You cannot afford to run short of money in the middle of your campaign. It will slow the process and cranking it all up again after an interim time lapse is not easy. It may be impossible to get back the original energy and focus.

It takes everything you have to begin the first time. Message:
Be prepared!

Chapter 9 illustrates the beginning of a strategic thinking and contemporary marketing strategy components, whose tools will be helpful in designing and implementing a successful job search campaign. You must see yourself as the marketer of *you.*

There is no better person or agency to do it. You are the only one who knows what you want in your first career position. It is possible to attain it. Plan and strategize as if you had the newest product on the market in your field. In reality you do. You are the one they are looking to hire. You have the most current education achievement. You are state of the art. You are the candidate who is the best prepared in your field. Go for it!

Chapter 8 Challenges

Technological

1. Chart how many people are a part of your marketing campaign, including those you hope to meet through the campaign completion.
2. Build a calendar that illustrates as many interview openings as you think you can handle successfully. In addition include time to write letters, do research, set appointments, formulate and send thank-you notes, and continue on a forward progress toward your goal.
3. Develop a time line or a Gantt chart and show the research time, mileage, travel means, allotted interview time, interview evaluation time, campaign assessment, and your progress toward a successful campaign resolution.
4. If you design a Web page, how many "hits" did you get, and have you incorporated design and executable time to do this on your time line from the third challenge?
5. Continue to use the Internet and the Web to stay current with business profiles, salary guides, and competitive résumés.
6. Chart your best scenario and identify priorities in terms of job acceptance criteria. The chart in chapter 6, page 61, could be helpful to you.
7. Design a visual that depicts the four Ps in your individual marketing strategy.
8. Check InfoTrac and ProQuest for company statistics and the most recent information.
9. Design your own marketing plan within a worldview. Evaluate your perceptions by checking your visual with one of your friends or a member of your support group.
10. Chart IRS rules about job searches, the costs, and their proper accounting for tax purposes.

Traditional

1. What are the four Ps of marketing and how would they help market you?
2. Of the various internal forces affecting your success in the market, which one gives you the most confidence? Which one could be a real roadblock to your success? How will you handle both of these factors to achieve your market aims?
3. Develop a plan to maximize the factor with which you are confident and build a supportive base so the anticipated roadblock is not effective.
4. Do the same for the external factors. Which ones are well in your control and which ones scare you? Develop a strategy to overcome the scary ones and use those already in your hands to advantage.
5. Outline the decisions you are prepared to make about these external factors. Then separate them from the ones about which you feel uneasy or hesitant to make decisions. You may need assistance from your support group members here. Take advantage of their wisdom and ask for advice and direction. Learn to identify your resources early in your campaign.
6. Create a career focus that will take you beyond your career objective.
7. Realistically assess the costs of a search in today's market and in your career field.
8. Estimate whether the cost of research and connections to the Internet and the Web are beneficial to your goal attainment.

Vocabulary

From the following list, select and explain the strictly marketing terms. Select and explain the strictly job search terms. How are they related?

advertising	disposition	personality
aims	expertise	place
analysis	external factors	policies
assessment	focus	price
attitude	four Ps	product
budget	individuality	promotion
campaign	internal factors	résumé
career search	interviews	salary range
communication	IRS	strategy
competition	job searching	tools
decision making		worldview

Chapter 9

INTERNAL FACTORS AFFECTING ACHIEVEMENT OF MARKET AIMS

LEARNING OBJECTIVES

After you study this chapter, you should be able to

- Know yourself in a more integrated way.
- Describe yourself, your general disposition, and your attitude toward the field you have chosen in positive terms.
- Know when your disposition is showing and whether it is positive for you and the observer.
- Determine your best personality characteristics and then put your best foot forward.
- Assess when you are under stress and plan for a way to handle the stress and yourself.

- Respect your knowledge and be able to communicate appropriate answers to interviewers' questions.
- Talk coherently about the specific focus of your degree and know why you pursued it.
- Relate your experience to your skill base, your degree, and your knowledge base.
- Consider your school time, lectures, laboratory work, and projects as valuable in your learning as any other work you may have done along the way.

LEARNING PROCESSES / SKILLS

PERSONAL FACTORS TO CONSIDER

Attitude
Disposition
Control Issues

PERSONALITY

Individuality
Reactions
Qualified Candidacy

KNOWLEDGE

Problem Solving
Performance
Tests

DEGREE

Level of Degree Earned
Subject of Major
Significant Courses
Important Laboratory Courses
Projects
Honors

EXPERIENCE

Paid/Volunteer Work
School Assignments
Hobbies
Skills

Got a chip on your shoulder? Has anyone ever told you that you have a bad attitude? So you have a degree, what do you know how to do? How much business experience do you have? What skills do you have? These are questions that get at the heart of chapter 9. Many interviewers, friends, associates, and business colleagues may approach you with these questions and then wait for your response. These are questions you need to be prepared to answer straightforwardly and logically. You cannot afford to be argumentative about these issues. This takes preparation and sensitivity.

■ *ATTITUDE*

One's attitude or disposition is gleaned in a variety of ways. Good interviewers are masters at getting you to reveal your attitude. It tells them about the way you will or will not fit into their company or department where they plan to place you. A well-degreed candidate can sparkle and dazzle with knowledge and creative, innovative answers to ways of handling different situations that might come up in a day's work. But none of this reveals your disposition or attitude toward work, management, peers, customers, or the company itself.

It is the job of the company interviewer to make an assessment about your disposition and your attitudes toward various components that might surface in a work situation. Tone of voice, manner of speaking or not speaking, directness or indirectness in your answers, facial expressions, body carriage, personal grooming, and enthusiasm all can be determined through body language. They can be read by sharp interviewers, and you need to send the right message about your attitude. No company needs or wants a person with a poor attitude.

Your disposition is always showing, so you need to be prepared to show off your best side at all times while job searching. What should you do on a bad day? First, acknowledge it. What went wrong? How do you feel? Why are you tired? What went awry? Know what has put you in a bad mood. Everyone else will soon know, if you do not become aware of it first. Then, if you know how you are feeling, you can take steps to change the way you feel, or plan to be extra careful and alert not to let the bad attitude or disposition raise its nasty head in public. This takes planning and a lot of personal insight.

If you are one of the world's "perfect" people who never have a bad day, then you are in for a surprise. Your disposition will step out and bite you and others when you least expect it. This is under your control as few other obstacles in a career search campaign are, so take charge. Practice meditation, learn tai chi, exercise more, plan less-stressful activity for the day in question, and eat carefully. All of these practices usually help in one way or another in coping with an occasional down day.

The internal factor of stress is introduced here because you can be the first person to notice the signs you may have dealt with this before so you know what to do. You are in control of this vacillating factor that accompanies career search campaigns. You are not in control of an individual you may meet who is in a malevolent mood, but you are in control of what you will do in case you are feeling irritable. Know yourself before others learn about you.

■ *PERSONALITY*

Personality is personal and individual to each of us. Happily we can be in control of the personality's manifestation to the outside world, unless we are in serious mental trouble. Individuality is one of the things you can control in conversation with another, and it also separates you from all others pursuing the same job option. Reworking individuality to your advantage is crucial to assure you a head start to the finish line.

Personality can look like arrogance in the hands of an amateur. But then arrogance is its own punishment, so you will either learn or be forever looked over to the candidate behind you. Depression is sometimes hidden but can be spotted by the astute observer. Some interviewers like to ask nervous people questions because they want to see their spontaneous reactions. They may not care what you say but rather how you say it. They are looking for individuation between you and another candidate.

Such questions include the following: Have you ever been angry with any of your previous bosses? Over what? How could you have handled it better? What are your weaknesses? From whom do you seek counsel when you are stymied by another person's behavior at work? Some issues, such as your attitudes about drunkenness, loud talk, unseemly jokes, or whining, have nothing to do with the job and its responsibilities.

What is an interviewer trying to uncover with these questions? Your reaction. It is possible no one cares about your answer; all they want is to see you react to emotionally charged situations or vocabulary. This tells them more about you than all the degrees you show on your résumé, all the philosophical explanations for why you want the position, and all the skill bases you can synthesize for use in the position. What they are looking for is your individuality, your personality, under stress.

Often in today's well-educated pool of talent in the workforce, several candidates may all have the credentials desired for a certain position. But there is only one position. Candidates assume that companies continue on the same plane as the interviewers begin to make their decisions. This is not true. As the interview process deepens, so do the questions interviewers want to investigate.

Here is something to remember when you do not get the job and you know you were qualified for the position. The decision makers went to another level to make their decisions about which one of the three qualified candidates they would hire. This is where the network interviewing with decision makers pays advance warning to you.

If you ask decision makers before you are a job candidate how they would make such decisions, you will learn a variety of methods they use. Some may jokingly say they throw the three résumés in the air and whichever lands right side up becomes their choice. Some will say they are looking for one with a "good disposition," whatever that means. And others will say, "When things are that close I'll pick someone with a sense of humor," and so on.

Knowing this will keep you from becoming discouraged when you are not selected and you know you were a qualified candidate. It will also challenge you to keep yourself on a full and active campaign, allowing nothing short of the actual job being offered to you and your accepting the same to slow your campaign drive. This awareness allows you to understand that you cannot afford to slow your campaign or to stray from your marketing aims.

Individuality is crucial to your being offered a position. It is also under your control. How you portray yourself to the interviewer will lead to or away from your candidacy for that position. Put on the interviewer's shoes for a while and imagine how it is to meet you in a job interview. If you have a good friend or relative who knows you pretty well, ask him or her how you look, appear, seem, even sound. Listen carefully to what he or she says. It could influence your candidacy for the best job available.

■ KNOWLEDGE

Knowledge is the state of knowing something. It implies a familiarity or understanding about a subject that was gained through experience or study. Some may call this erudition. Unfortunately your degree does not guarantee your future employer that you know a lot about your field of study. However, your degree can be a signal as to your interest in a field, some subjective judgments of professors in the field about your expertise, and a college's evaluation concerning a rigorous curriculum and your measurement against its completion. That is about all it says. You have to be able to demonstrate your knowledge and level of expertise aside from your degree.

Companies have varieties of ways to investigate your knowledge in light of what they expect you to be able to do for them. Some use standard tests; others use their own homegrown varieties of tests. Some ask for computer skills application by giving you a real or imagined problem to solve. They watch how you go about solving the problem and may not be at all interested in your answers. In each case you need to ask where and when you will receive the evaluation of your performance on the test.

Some companies ask you to submit to personality inventories to see whether you would fit into the company's culture. It would be well if you had already figured that one out for yourself through research into the company culture. Why would you be interviewing for a position in a company whose culture is unknown or opposite your interests and values? That aside, you need to be most careful about what tests you agree to take.

You can know whether it is a standardized or company-specific test; you can also know why the test is significant and a requirement of all candidates. Ask when, where, and with whom you will go over the results of this testing. If the test is nonstandardized, pass. If there is no evaluation method revealed to you, pass. You do not need this company. Either it is too nosy about its employees or incompetent in dealing with an educated workforce. In either case you need to go on to the next option.

This is private information you are sharing with the company. If it does not know how to respect your privacy, then it becomes your responsibility to protect your own privacy. Your response might be that you have nothing to hide. We all hope not, but that does not give a company the implicit right to mess around with your head and dig into your privacy without demonstrating cause or relevance to the position you are seeking to fill.

◼ *DEGREE*

What does a degree say? Unfortunately, not much today. This is not the same as saying the degree is worthless. What a degree means is largely a mystery to all who read about it on a résumé and a hard-earned shield for those who have earned one. What makes its mixed reputation so puzzling is the area of study and what that might mean.

Colleges used to graduate only bachelor of arts candidates with a major in philosophy or fine arts. Eventually bachelor of science degrees started to proliferate, and they implied a minimum of humanities courses and an emphasis on scientific courses. Then degrees became distinguished in a variety of fields with a major emphasis.

Knowledge doubles and triples in some industries within three to five years. Therefore specialties had to be created within the academic communities for them to remain credible in their assessments, evaluations, and granting a variety of degrees to candidates who had studied within their curriculum guidelines. Today, one degree means different things depending on the college, the curriculum, and what accrediting agencies say about the college and its right to grant degrees.

Your degree is only as valuable as its perception in the marketplace. If you have a new subject degree, B.S. (telecommunications management), what does that mean? Do you have a management degree or a technical degree in the field of telecommunications? What does the degree certify you can do? Because it is not clear, it is important that you list with more specificity what your education credential represents on your résumé (see chapter 4). What theory courses were significant, what seminars were important, and what projects enabled you to best show you understood the theory enough to make it work in a project?

How your résumé looks in the section on education is in your hands. You earned the degree, so you are the most qualified to say what it represented to you by way of knowledge gained and skills acquired or improved, as well as ways you have already used it in your various projects throughout your education process and in your work. This is under your control. The way you respond to this piece of background data will help or hinder you in achieving your market aims.

◼ *WORK EXPERIENCE*

Work experience can be before and during your college degree pursuit. Experience can be gained by working and receiving remuneration for it, or it can be volunteer work for which a different kind of recognition may be given. The employer needs to see whether you have experience. Are you familiar enough with the information, the challenges, the opportunities of the future in your chosen field?

Experience is usually far more focused than education and often why employers are more willing to talk about experience than education. Education is broad-based arrangement of knowledge in a certain field. Education explains the why and wherefore of process or theory. Experience says, "Do it this way," and unfortunately sometimes adds, "and don't ask why."

College laboratory assignments are experience and should not be ignored just because they were the outcome of an educational assignment. Often projects that accompany class theory are where the real learning takes place, because the theory becomes real to the student in the exercise. Learning how to make real your experience in laboratory situations while you earned your degree is a challenge, but you are up to it and only you can do it.

Skills are more numerous than anything else in each college graduate's credentials. You have just completed a rigorous program that resulted in a degree. There are so many skills you have exercised and improved over the course of your degree that it would be hard to list all of them. Examine carefully what you have selected for your skills profile and keyword stripe on your résumé.

These skills are what you are highlighting for a potential employer. Do the skills you have chosen to list reveal your best and most significant skills? Employers assume listed skills are accomplished skills, not wish lists of some skills you hope to have one day. Skills are translated as expertise by the résumé reader. Make sure your list is accurate.

Everyone can improve on any skill or set of skills. However, when you put them on your résumé they are presumed an achievement of a distinguished level and that you are ready to use these skills when you hit the floor running in your new position. You know to what degree you possess these skills, so honestly reflect that in the skills profile and on the keyword stripe.

The internal factors that affect achievement of your market aims are all within your power and control. Understand this about yourself. Speak honestly about your attitude, personality, knowledge, degree, experience, and skill levels. This is not the time for modesty unless you translate modesty as truth. Use these internal factors about which you have primitive consciousness. Be sophisticated in the way you use these factors on your own behalf. Only you can do the best job of representation in this category.

Chapter 9 Challenges

Technological

1. Chart your personal growth from the first moment of consciousness for you to current self-awareness and identify the important influences along the way.
2. Be sure you can talk about your degree roots, your college history, and your choices with enthusiasm. Know what distinguishes your alma mater from other colleges. Practice with your peers, support group members, and interested others.
3. Practice delivering before a mirror how your degree separates you from others with your age and experience wanting to get into a new career field. Videotape your performance. Then go back and listen to the tape while you evaluate your performance. Repeat this often so that you get better and better at projecting your enthusiasm about your college choice and your degree field. Check it out with your support group members.
4. Why should an employer hire you? Display on a chart and explain to someone in your support group why you think this. Use the chart.
5. Take the personality inventory in appendix F and illustrate the results on a graph. Do you think the inventory results are accurate for you? Why?
6. How well do you know yourself? Design a chart of characteristics that reflect the best in your personality. Rate yourself on a basis of 100 percent. Is the result anything like the real you?

Traditional

1. Assess your attitude and figure out how you would state your disposition accurately. After you said it, would your presentation have helped or hindered your chances of being employed in the field of your choice? Try this on someone who knows you and who will be honest with you about what you present. Listen to the feedback.
2. Prepare a set of questions that you would find difficult or troublesome to answer. Then build good and confident answers to those questions. Remember how confident you were about these answers if they come up in an interview and repeat the answer again with purpose and enthusiasm.

3. Imagine your reaction to being turned down for a position for which you were qualified. What would be your reaction toward the decision maker? with your support group members? and by yourself at the end of that day?

4. Imagine being told you were not an acceptable candidate for a position because you appear too grouchy or unfriendly. What could you do to overcome that assessment, then and there, and in future interviews?

5. How well do you know yourself? Write a short biographical sketch for a future employer to read before you are hired. What personal characteristics will you highlight? Share with peers, friends, family, and possibly colleagues. What do they say? How do they react?

Vocabulary

Select fifteen words and build a relational frame in which to put them.

aim	education	personality
assessment	experience	personality inventories
attitude	individuality	project
campaign	job search	résumé
candidate	keyword stripe	skills
company culture	knowledge	skills profile
decision maker	laboratory course	tai chi
degree	meditation	theory
disposition		worldview

Chapter 10

EXTERNAL FACTORS AFFECTING ACHIEVEMENT OF MARKET AIMS

LEARNING OBJECTIVES

After you study this chapter, you should be able to

- More accurately assess the work markets and conditions within your career choice.
- Distinguish between and among factors over which you have no control and factors over which you have control.
- Research the companies of interest to you by using the Internet, ProQuest, InfoTrac, libraries' directories, and so on.
- Develop a complete business portfolio for the companies that interest you.

- Study and research the state of the economy.
- Compare the various environments in which you may work.
- Discern the attitude of employees in the companies that have your interest.
- Develop a questioning mind when researching a company, its management, and its workforce.
- Approach outside areas that you can control by making decisions.
- Make decisions with confidence in your ability to do so.

LEARNING PROCESSES / SKILLS _____

COMPLEX SITUATIONS

Company Politics
Job Competition
Company Culture
Litigation History
General Economy
Congressional Law
New Technology
Sense of History

OUTSIDE FACTORS YOU CAN CONTROL

Interview Process
Developing Job Leads
Communication Patterns

Decision-Making Ability
Professionalism

DECISION MAKING

Game Theory
Analysis
Research
Methodology
Leadership
Communication
Interviews
Job Leads
Seeing Relationships
Charting Information
Prioritizing

There are external factors that will affect the outcome of your job search. You can and will know about them but cannot control the factors in any way other than your attitude. From the last chapter you can see how important attitude is. In addition, there are immediate circumstances within a job search campaign that are in your control, but they are external factors affecting the outcome of the campaign.

■ COMPLEX SITUATIONS

First, let us look at the external factors over which you have no control other than your attitude about them. These include knowledge about your competitors for the position you want and company policies for the firm you want to join. Generally these factors would be considered unknown and out of the control of the searcher, but you know better.

You can evaluate your competition by looking at résumés that are similar to yours on the Internet. It does not cost much to look. Compare your credentials with others and then plan your attack. Knowing a company's policies is a matter of including some of the company's employees in your network interviewing and asking them what you want to know. They will not give you a company manual, but most employees have little compunction about revealing what they consider to be the company's policies toward potential employees.

Although these are basically unknown factors to most candidates, you have the insight and the methods of getting the answers you need to affect your campaign positively. These matters are not out of your control, nor need they be unknown to you. Business profiles, interviewing, and market assessment are tools available to you through the Internet and your own ingenuity. Business profiles can be downloaded to disks or printed in libraries with dedicated Internet PCs.

ProQuest makes CD-ROMs available for general and business information gathering to assist with research about a company and its policies. InfoTrac is another CD-ROM service with a significant distinction; one CD-ROM is available for magazine and journal articles, and another CD-ROM is dedicated to business profiles.

More and more technology becomes available almost daily, so keep your eyes open for what will help you the most. Ask the librarian for the services and resources he or she can put at your service. Remember that the librarian is the most qualified person who knows where everything is in the library and under what heading it can be accessed for your use.

As you are making yourself more and more knowledgeable about the competition and the nature of the businesses that interest you, do not be overwhelmed by the mass amount of data or discouraged by the challenge the data may present you. Data should be analyzed and used to your best advantage. Be careful when accumulating so much information that you have a way of considering how useful the data may be to you.

There are also known but complicated factors that will affect achievement of your goal. The economy, environment, society, technology, politics, and law all affect the possible success of your marketing campaign. You can know about each of these elements and how they might affect your campaign, but you are virtually powerless to change anything within these areas before your job search completion.

It is important to note here that taking on anything other than your job search will distract your focus and disturb your momentum. Any activity to affect these above listed six areas will only dissipate your energies and slow your campaign success. What you really are doing is a job search. The other issues can wait.

An example would be if you ran into an interviewer who was sexist or racist, maybe subtly or overtly. You might have the option of a lawsuit "to bring the individual to justice," but then where would you find the time to do that if you are in a full-blown job search? Move on to other companies in your own search. You could take this individual to court and you may win your point, but you still will not have the job you are searching for. Stay focused.

■ *RESEARCH*

What to do about the economy? Read about it. Know how it affects your industry directly or indirectly. Be conversant about the distinctions that need to be drawn, because they make a difference. Seek advice and counsel about the future of economic trends as perceived by those who profess to have such knowledge.

This is not a big-time research project for you, but you need the information to guide your approach to the marketplace of your choice. You need this information to make decisions about your own campaign and how effective you can be in using this knowledge to advantage. Again, stay focused. You need the information, but not so much as will move the market one way or another. You need these data for your own purposes.

The environment encompasses the outside environment, as well as the internal environment, of a company structure. Does the company do anything that violates the environment where its plants and outlets are situated? How does it dispose of waste? Where does it put discretionary funds to help environmental concerns improve? If you are not interested in this, at least be aware of your potential employer's attitude toward the issue. It could play a part in your decision to accept a job with a company.

Then you must consider the environment within the company itself. Is it inviting and comfortable? Do people seem to have whatever they need to do their jobs successfully? Are the laws concerning human resources management and labor relations observed? Do people say they are paid adequately for their services? Are company departments competitive or cooperative in their interrelationship?

What is the feel of the atmosphere in which you hope to be working? Take the temperature of the workplace. You will be in it for a long time if you accept a position with the company. One-third of each day, week, month, and year will be spent here. Consider that in your deliberations and assessment of a company's environment.

Society is probably the oldest catalyst of management change within organizations. It is not the only factor, but it has a lot of sway when it comes to why businesses are tolerated in neighborhoods, companies are given tax breaks to come into a city, and business production is respected by the community. People want to know about the positive contribution the company makes to the cultural life of the society. These are all ways society measures participation of a business in the growth and development of communities.

How can you know what influences a city or society to accept or reject any given company? Do research in back issues of the local newspaper. Herein lie the tales that led the city to accept certain companies into its limits while it refused or expelled others. Bring these factors into your inquiry while doing network interviewing to add breadth and depth to your awareness.

Listen to what people say. Some know a lot about the history of a company being accepted into a community. Others know very little. It is your job to find out as much as you need to know to satisfy your campaign goal and to help you make a decision about accepting or rejecting a position offer.

Technology is probably the most recent and effective mover of businesses today. It is important that the companies you are considering as potential employers have entered the computer age.

The industrial age is over; the job remains an icon of the industrial age. The icon of the computer age is the PC or laptop. Where on this scale is the business you are researching?

Look around when you are interviewing. Talk to the employees and listen to how they tell the story of their company's growth or lack of it. People will give you lots of information if you ask the right questions and gain their confidence. Why do this? You need the data to make an informed decision, should a position be offered to you.

Politics of the nation, the state, the county, and the city are all in place to assist the citizens in governing themselves in our democratic society. Laws are passed by elected representatives at all these levels regarding what the society is willing to accept in the behavior of others in a free nation. What has the market done that engages politicians and legislatures in formulating laws to govern business activities?

This obviously is a matter of history. It is also a matter of contemporary civics. No informed professional can be ignorant about how the government is run in a free society. A free society does not govern business or business's operations. It governs the people and their free access to the markets entrepreneurs can develop and proffer. In the ideal state all works together in harmony.

We do not live in the ideal state, and so you must know how the government works with business and how business works within the government's laws. Ignorance is never a defense for breaking the law. Most companies have in-house legal departments or hire lawyers as needed to protect them from breaking the laws accidentally and to defend them against anyone who chooses to bring litigation against the company.

Can you know if a company has litigation pending against it and what that litigation is? Yes. You can ask directly, read the 10K report, and keep current with business journals and business commentary in the electronic media. You can know what litigation is pending, its current status, and who filed the suit, whether management, employees, customers, vendors, suppliers, government agencies, competition, or others.

This alone will tell you volumes about the company and its relationships with the various stakeholders interested in its success. You need to know this because it is part of the data you are building on a company of your choice to determine whether it is the best place to begin your career.

Remember that your career and name are unsullied. It makes no sense to unite them with a company that has a mottled business reputation and is in litigation.

Litigation alone is not enough for you to stop considering the company. You need to know who is involved in the litigation. You need to know in what stage the litigation is and its probable outcome. And you need to read some commentary about how this litigation is perceived by the competitors of the company and scholars who spend hours analyzing such matters.

Writing about these conflicts and situations in business appears in scholarly journals such as the *Harvard Business Review*. These are often translated into business language for magazines including *FORTUNE* Magazine or some trade journals of repute. This information is of great vocational interest to business scholars.

Even though you cannot change policies and practices in the economy, environment, society, technology, politics, and law, you need to know what is happening in these areas to make your search credible and effective. These known factors are complicated and out of your control, but they will affect the outcome of your search in one way or another. Knowledge will enable you to make a more informed decision than if you blindly ignore what is happening in the culture.

■ *CONTROL FACTORS*

You ask what external factors are in your control, if any. There are four: interviews, job leads, communication patterns, and decision-making procedures. These are definitely in your control. They are the more immediate circumstances of your job search campaign and will call for your attention more often. However, they must be seen in light of the other external factors to enable you to find the best position possible.

Interviews are yours to schedule and enjoy. You select whom you will see, determine what kind of interview it will be, and analyze the effectiveness after the fact. It is totally in your control in all its aspects. If you blow it, it is your fault. You cannot blame anyone else. The information you attain in these interviews will be as high-powered and helpful as your questions are sharp and focused on what you want to know. None of us has time to waste. Neither do any of the people you want to interview. Keep it short, simple, and focused, and the information will be incredibly helpful to you. You called the meeting; the agenda is yours.

Job leads will come from all of the interviews you schedule. For obvious reasons, you do not want to ask for outside job leads if you are interviewing for a job within the company. If you do not get the job, then ask for leads to other people in the industry and about any other opportunities the individual may know. Most are willing to help you. Also ask at that time what he or she thinks of your interviewing style, what suggestions the interviewer might offer that would help make you more successful the next time, and why you were not chosen, unless you already know.

All other interviews can be concluded with comments about what your research has uncovered. Include a request for help with job leads and access to other professionals in the field, as well as other companies of similar design and purpose. You want basic leads to assist you in finding the best position possible for you. You will find that if you stay clear about your reason for asking for an interview people will be willing to help you in any way they can. If you pull a bait-and-switch tactic you will be history, fast.

Communication is a matter of style as well as substance. Some people are warm and inviting, and it is a pleasure to meet and talk with them. Others are stilted, unsure of themselves, and open to criticism, even ridicule, because they seem so inept. There is a vast continuum between these two extremes. Your work is to move as quickly as you can to the style that people like.

Treating people as you would like to be treated is a good place to begin. Next, observe what you see people doing as they talk with you. What is the manner of the person you are interviewing? What kind of an atmosphere does the individual set to make you comfortable? Remember these little things. They could be the make-or-break decision point with an interviewer down the line who must make a decision among three qualified candidates for the one available position.

■ DECISION MAKING

The power to make decisions requires knowledge, ability to assess and evaluate data, judgment, and courage. You will be the recipient of whatever you decide to accept. Your decision marks the beginning of a new career. This choice should make you feel fulfilled in all your pursuits to this point. You have spent money and time, sacrificed good times, burned the midnight oil before exams, and made sacrifices of personal pleasure to secure funding for your goals. Now is no time to fall down on your determination to secure the best possible position.

When making your decisions about which job offers are the best, measure them all against the criteria you developed on page 61 in chapter 6. Align each position of top priority to you, side by side with the others, and measure which job is the best option for you at the moment of your decision. You cannot make a decision based on how this will play ten years from now. Your decision is in the present, and you need to evaluate the criteria in the same time frame.

Decision making can be scary, but not if you have been careful up to this point. Assess the value of your information and measure how close it gets you to your dream job. Not everyone gets their dream job, but most are able to come very close. Compare salary with salary across the options available to you. Compare benefits packages against what you developed for yourself on page 61. Compare job satisfaction factors across the options. This is the only way you can be fair to yourself.

You might try using the *Game Theory* option described in chapter 6 and adapt it as part of your own decision-making processes. Designate the weight each of these factors has for you. You did this when you negotiated; bring the process out again and compare your offers on an even playing field. Take your time. You can repent in leisure if you make the wrong decision. If you are frightened of decision making, bring in a member of your support group to assist you. Pick someone in the group who really has your best interest at heart.

Learning how to make decisions is another set of skills that requires practice. Everyone can learn to make good decisions if they will just take their time and analyze the consequences of their decisions. Few decisions are irrevocable. By practicing different styles of decision making you will soon arrive at what works the best for you.

Some people are very logical and need charts laid out in linear paths with Roman numerals, capital letters under the Roman numerals, Arabic numerals under the capital letters, and lowercase letters under the Arabic numerals. It is very clear to them where the choices lie and which ones would be most beneficial.

Others can use visual methods for making their decisions. Plot the information on various charts that can be viewed simultaneously to "see" the decision that is most appropriate for the situation. Graphing data is helpful here. If you are familiar with graphics interfaces and software packages you probably know just how you will visualize your next decision.

Some make decisions quickly because it feels right for them. This may appear a dangerous method for the logical decision maker. And it is, but it may not be a problematic method for free-spirited decision makers, because this is the way they make decisions all the time. Most of the time the decisions are right for them.

Being a person who can make decisions makes others feel more at ease. Taking responsibility for making others comfortable is a mark of a gracious individual and a confident person.

You need to discover what works best for you. Try a variety of methods and improve on the one that seems right for you. Sometimes the situation itself calls for a different style of decision making. Do some research and it will not be long before you feel comfortable with a new method of decision making.

If you have difficulty making decisions at all, never apply for leadership and managerial positions because you will only cause chaos. Force yourself to make decisions consciously about little things until you gain some confidence in decision making. It helps to remember that if you do not like the results of the decision, you probably can change them with another decision. Again, you must discover the style of decision making that gives you comfort, as well as good decisions.

These immediate circumstances are totally in your control. Interviews, job leads and how you follow them, communication style, and decision-making capability are all external but in your control. Take charge. You can do it. You have earned it.

Chapter 10 has illustrated how it is possible to have goals and factors working against the goals but not defeating them. This is not in the factors themselves but in the job searcher's ability to take charge of what truly can be managed. Learn as much as you can about that over which you have no control. Select how best to tune your attitude in order to make the most of the data received to accomplish your own goal.

Chapter 8 looked at what is in your control to achieve your market aims: the evolution and design of the résumé, the ability to analyze the situation of the marketplace for your chosen profession, the sharpness of your career focus, the development of a marketing strategy that will reward you with great options for choosing, and a budget that will support your search for as long as you need to find what you want.

Chapter 9 looked inside you for the personal factors that you have to use in the achievement of your goals. Your attitude and disposition, your personality and individuality, your accumulated knowledge, your earned degree, your experience and familiarity with the field, and your skills and expertise are what matter in the way the potential employer sees you. You are in charge of all those things. Be good to and fair with yourself. Avoid negative criticism of yourself because it will drain your energy.

Chapter 10 has pointed out the external factors that could be obstacles, but they will not be problems for you. You know what you can and cannot change. The usual mystery behind knowing who your competitors are can be alleviated by Internet research. Company policies can be known through network interviews. You have the tools to find the information.

External factors over which you have no control but about which you are knowledgeable are the major factors that move management decision making. These include the economy, the internal and external environmental issues, the society in which you live, the technology and how it continues to develop, and the political framework of the country.

All politics is local. Understand that and you are well on your way to becoming an informed citizen in a free society.

The immediate circumstances that you will face every day of your search are interviews, whom to see, where and why, and following job leads. Which interviews are more significant than others? How well are you communicating your goals? Are you improving with each planned interview and all chance encounters? Are you honing your decision-making skills? All of this is under your control, so take charge and succeed at finding your first career position.

Chapter 10 Challenges

Technological

1. Use the Internet to identify your competition and to build current business profiles.
2. Use the Internet's newsgroups to get a daily understanding of the economy, your career field, and the local and distant environments that affect your career.
3. Use the technology available to search, to decide, to evaluate your best options, to put your résumé before the right decision maker's eyes, twenty-four hours a day, seven days a week.
4. Create a job criteria sheet comparable to the one in chapter 6, page 61, but be specific to your personal job search campaign.
5. Translate *Game Theory* into decision making and weight the values related to your decisions.

Traditional

1. List all of the external factors affecting your achievement of the market aims and put an appropriate strategy opposite each one you list.
2. Design a way to maximize your internal factors to help you reach your market aims more quickly.
3. Study the factor of decision making and design a path for yourself that will assure that you are making appropriate and right decisions most of the time.
4. Identify three ways you might overcome the following extrinsic factors to your success in meeting your market aims: economics of your field, society in which you live, company culture where you work, and competition for the position.
5. Make a list of recommendations, based on observations of your classmates and their success or lack of it in finding a good job. Take these data to the graduate-placement office or its equivalent in your school. Your purpose is both to solicit their help and attention and to give some aid and comfort to your classmates.

Vocabulary

Build a crossword puzzle to share with your classmates. Use thirty to thirty-five words. Use clear definitions for the columns and rows.

aims	computer age	industrial age	network
assessment	decision making	Internet	policies
attitude	dream job	interviews	politics
benefits package	economy	job leads	reputation
budget	electronic media	job satisfaction	résumés
business profiles	entrepreneurs	job search	skills
campaign	environment	knowledge	society
CD-ROMs	external factors	law	strategy
communication	*FORTUNE*	litigation	style
company policies	*Game Theory*	marketplace	technology
competition	*Harvard Business Review*	negotiation	10K report

Segment 4

CONTEMPORARY CONSIDERATIONS

Most of this book has been dedicated to the job search campaign itself. This segment is an integral part of your job search; job searching continues after you are employed in your dream job. Segment 4 is about the future and your responsibility for becoming aware of the changes in yourself, your profession, and your dreams.

Understand the technical side of continuing development and how it will be helpful to the profession you have chosen. This is imperative for you. Use technology's innovations in software packages and hardware development, which will double every three or four years or more often. Expand your accumulated skill bases. Chapter 11 will assist you with this basic self-knowledge.

You must be aware of the best way to market yourself, which is to know your skills and be able to restate them in the terminology of the field where you are or the field you want to enter. Think of yourself as a provider of useful skills that you can describe in practical language for function-oriented field managers and division leaders so that they may understand more coherently how you can best help them achieve their goals and objectives.

Chapter 12, on the other hand, supports those who want to concentrate on working as entrepreneurs. This choice needs a lot of research and information so that the selector will be as well informed as possible about the ramifications of this decision and the devastating outcomes this entrepreneurial choice may generate. Entrepreneurs are a rare breed of business persons. It would be important to know someone who has started a business and been as successful as possible in that business.

The downside is that 90 percent of new businesses fail in the first year of operation. So you can see that it will not be easy.

Chapter 12 includes a short inventory to assess your interest and background for such a venture. Learn how to do appropriate research into entrepreneurship. This is as vital as actually making the decision to plunge into your own business. It is not easy, and it will only become more difficult as you develop and grow with your business.

You will have different challenges than if you worked for someone else, and your challenges will vary from those of established companies. There is a lot to learn before you make this decision;

steps are identified about your entrepreneurial decision. Doing things in a disciplined and informed manner will help assure that you do not end up among the 90 percent.

Small business itself is a deep pool of information, tips, guidelines, and support for making your decision or changing your mind and deciding to work for someone else. Would-be entrepreneurs abound in our country. Successful entrepreneurs are less numerous. Wealthy and successful entrepreneurs are the fewest in numbers.

Nevertheless, entrepreneurs can assist you with your search. The Better Business Bureau is a good source for people to contact for information and guidance. The federal government has an organization called the Service Corps of Retired Executives (SCORE) within the ranks of the Small Business Administration (SBA). These people have all been successful entrepreneurs and business managers and are capable of giving good advice. You will not lack for good advice and counsel. The question is whether you will seek and accept it.

Job security is the most sought after illusion that people consider while job searching. There is no such thing as job security. Chapter 13 makes that point and describes various alternatives you can explore to learn to accept yourself as your own security. You need to have confidence in the services or products you can provide.

Today's marketplace is a different work world than even the 1970s and the 1980s were for your older brothers and sisters or your parents. It certainly is vastly different from what your grandparents experienced. The marketplace is going to keep changing while you are working. There are no guarantees with your degree, your skill base, your education, or your work experience.

Your job is not secure. The business for which you work is not secure. The demand the market will make for your skills is not secure. The workplace is a pretty shaky place. Some comfort may reside in the fact that it is just as shaky for everyone. Change is hard to manage and enjoy.

Does this sound problematic or what?

The job concept is an industrial age icon and does not apply in most of today's workplaces or to contemporary workers. Cyberspace is no place for job security. Internet connections and speedy travel through space have changed the workplace decidedly. You will be called upon to rethink and possibly rename what you are looking for—a job or an opportunity to use your skills for someone else's benefit for a short time? Sometimes this may even be a single project, and after finishing it you will be expected to move on to something else.

This is where understanding how to market yourself and having good self-esteem and confidence in your developed skill bases, education, and work experience will come in handy, to say the least. Think of yourself as a constant searcher for people, businesses, and projects that need your skills, even though it may seem a bit unsettling. Nonetheless it is a realistic description of the workplace you are now entering. Chapter 13 will assist you to rethink your aspirations and review any antiquated notions you may have about job permanence or security.

A less-uncertain but viable option to consider is the possibility of in-house job searching. This would require the human resources personnel and your manager to know that you would like to be considered as a candidate for other work in the company when that option becomes available and you are qualified for the position. These people can be helpful and supportive of your moving on to bigger and better places in the company. It is always more profitable for a company to promote from within than to go outside to hire new people to fill existing positions that are above entry level.

Making political allies is crucial here. If you want to succeed in climbing the ladder to success in a company you need to play the political game to win. Plan, decide who is trustworthy, be your own counsel, and watch for opportunities with education, certificates of merit, course work, even a new degree, if that will boost your chances to go where you want to go in the company.

The last chapter introduces the topic of continuous job searching. You can never stop searching if you expect to remain competitive in your profession. Awareness of what the economy is doing and how it affects your field is a daily and weekly subject for research and discussion with other professional people. These issues are usually the subject of business lunches and trade or professional association meetings.

Marketing gets more and more sophisticated as technology advances. So will marketing yourself in the career of your choice. You will need constant contact with your network to stay above water in the changing environments of your current profession and any new ones you wish to enter. Keep your business portfolio updated monthly so that you will have some peace of mind. Then when people ask you for a résumé or business portfolio you will have one that is current. People make too many mistakes when they scramble to put a résumé together quickly. Keep your business portfolio updated and your supervisor informed at review time of your habit of updating your business portfolio.

When your manager receives a copy, explain that this is how you keep on top of the new skills and business practices you are learning in your position. This way you will prevent panic when the news arrives from somewhere else that you have a business portfolio. Your manager has already seen it, and there is a copy in your personnel file.

Professional membership in the best trade or business associations is imperative. It is where exchanges will be made and knowledge acquired about openings that are available. Business associations publish journals that describe current trends and often ways of taking advantage of the challenges of new situations. In addition the better associations will have workshops and guest speakers to assist their members to remain current within their own profession.

Networking (business breakfasts, power lunches, association dinners) can help you advance your career by making you aware of what is going on outside your own work cubicle. The temptation is to take the line of least resistance and stay in for lunch, have little or no contact with other professionals in your field, and keep your nose to the grindstone. Do not get stuck in such a rut; it is not necessary.

Chapter 11

TECHNICIAN AND TECHNOLOGY

LEARNING OBJECTIVES

After you study this chapter, you should be able to

- Talk confidently about your skills as if they were technical. For example, English major = wordsmith, researcher; history major = researcher, Internet specialist; music major = keyboard or instrumentalist, composer. Computer science and electronics technology are not the only fields that can claim specific skills.
- Be as computer literate as you can be with or without formal classes.

- Communicate and interact with others using the Internet, hardware, and software that are available.
- Use the Internet with confidence.
- Know that *technician* equals *skilled worker* and *knowledge worker* in an identified field or career.
- Monitor change and movement within your own career field.

LEARNING PROCESSES / SKILLS

TRANSLATION

Skills Consciousness
Translatable Options
Thesaurus
Where Are You Now?

COMPUTER LITERACY

Hardware Differentiation
Software Programs
Desktop Publishing

HISTORY OF ACADEMIC GROWTH

Philosophy Degree
Law Degree
Medical Degree
Arts and Letters
Science and Engineering
Technical Degree

INTERNET

Keyword Stripe
Skills Profile

Liberal arts graduates may bristle at this next concept, but bear in mind the marketplace you are entering with your degree. Earlier you were asked to consider yourself as a deliverer of services or skills to a business need. This may best be accomplished by thinking about what you know how to do within a technical framework. You are the translator of your skills, education, and experience. The employer is the evaluator of whether your skills, education, and experience will be useful in the position or business for which you are being chosen or considered.

◼ VOCABULARY TRANSLATION FOR BUSINESS LEADERS

You may call yourself a wordsmith rather than an English major; you could be a support, good listener, or tester rather than a psychology major; you might look at your work from a major in history as research skills. You may have some hard technical skills such as word processing, spreadsheet capability, graphics interface, and DOS. You are telling the tale. Get some help if you have difficulty with this activity so that your story is translated suitably for the markets you are considering for a position.

Appendix H lists words with which you may want to translate your skill base into a more technical frame. Be sure that you have selected what you want your résumé to reveal about yourself before looking for translatable options. Do not use any word for which you do not know the accurate meaning. Look words up in a dictionary or use a thesaurus to develop even more terms to describe what you are capable of doing for the reader of your résumé.

◼ HARDWARE/SOFTWARE ADVANTAGES

Being computer literate is critical to becoming a continuously growing skilled professional. In the past, everyone who was considered computer literate was able to use a word processor, a spreadsheet, and some graphics processing. All knew about DOS. The gurus also knew how to program, which immediately set them apart and, in their own eyes, above their colleagues.

Now it is important that you know how to do all that and also have taught yourself how to use a variety of word-processing software programs. There are usually several spreadsheet packages you may have learned at work or in school. Graphics are big because they enable the designer of a report to make it far more interesting to read with appropriate graphs and graphic illustrations.

Add to this the option of doing your work in color. Making your reports interesting by including some comedic cartoons or scanning information or pictures illustrates your skills as an accomplished desktop publisher. If you know the ins and outs of printers, it will make you a star in the office. And your degree may be in history or English, so you have many skills. Look them over carefully and figure out how to talk about your skills in a technical framework. This does not diminish or demean your degree but accents the breadth of your skill base.

Often graduates are unable to focus on their skills because they have no real assessment of them. The degree is expected to sell itself, and in this day and age it does not do that. Alphabet soup best describes the way universities and colleges catalog degrees. The areas of study are as diverse and complex as the institution dictates, but there is little or no clue about what the graduates know or what they can do.

Historical Sidebar

In an earlier age, when degrees were signs of advanced learning among a few chosen scholars, everyone knew that a Ph.D. was a degree in philosophy. The degree enabled the holder to be a teacher in that field. A master's degree indicated a certain in-depth proficiency within a field of choice such as English, literature, history, music, and so on.

It was clear what one had studied. A bachelor's degree was a sign of significant learning and represented not only an educated person but a professionally polished person ready for business or public discourse.

Later colleges and universities were forced to expand the options offered and develop curricula that reflected the needs of the times. There was much more to learn and more fields to cover if the institutions of learning were to be responsible for measuring an individual's knowledge or capability in one field or another and certifying that with a degree.

Today an individual who has earned a bachelor's degree in education does not have the same sets of skills as someone whose degree was granted ten years earlier, even though the degree still has the same value in the catalog. The two people were prepared differently for their field and may have widely different educations and perspectives on what their degrees mean.

This is even more traumatic if the degree is a technical degree in a field in which the knowledge base doubles or triples every four or five years. Individuals with the same degrees from the same institutions with the same majors will know vastly different things within the same field in as short a time as three or four years.

This is why it is so important that your résumé reveal what you think was significant about your theory courses, what seminars were helpful in developing the skills you want to use in your first career position, and how useful the projects were where you combined theory and practice into one venture. Once again you are the translator for the reader. Only you can make your background and credentials something the reader can understand. The title of your degree will not do this for you. You will have to become more involved in translating what your degree represents.

■ *NEW TECHNOLOGY DEVELOPMENT*

The Internet connections, by whatever server you use, will prove invaluable when it comes to knowing what is happening outside your own business and your own space in that business. Most professionals have their noses to the grindstone during their working hours and can become oblivious to what is happening outside their own career environments.

Be smart. Invest in the Internet as soon as you can. You will not regret this decision. Once you have access to the Internet, float your résumé or portfolio on the Internet. See what happens. You never know when you will get a better offer, but you will not get one if you do not put yourself out there.

You may wonder what will happen if your boss sees it. If you have already given your manager a copy of your business portfolio, then it has been read and filed in your personnel file. It will not shock your supervisor if someone calls and asks about your credentials and working habits. If your manager has not been advised that you update your business portfolio as a matter of course, there will be a problem. If this is a surprise, you have invited disaster.

On the other side of the issue, always ask individuals who are interested in you as a potential employee to treat your inquiry, business portfolio (and keep calling it your business portfolio), and any interviewing with them as confidential information. This is important because you could lose your job if your boss discovers that you are considering other options. Courtesy, as in all other fields of endeavor, will always help. Make it clear that you expect this confidentiality to be kept as a professional courtesy.

Continue to learn about software packages. One way to discover everything a software package can do for you is to take some time and make sure you understand every item listed under the titles on the menu bar. Many purchasers of software dislike reading the accompanying technical manual; you may find out more about your software than you knew existed by using this investigative approach.

Begin with the menu title at the far left of the menu bar and bring down the listed titles of what it will provide for you. Then click each option and see what happens. Gradually move from menu item to menu item until you reach the last one. If you have searched each of these titles thoroughly you will know the software package very well.

If you have a mouse, click the far right button and see what is revealed. Sometimes clicking the button twice rapidly will bring something else to your screen. On some mouse hardware there is a center button. See what it does. If you explore the options of this hardware you will become less afraid of the computer and its swiftness, because you are becoming more competent. Keep learning. This is what makes you a valuable employee. Next begin to use some of this knowledge in your work or private life. Like all skills, computer skills get better with practice.

Think of yourself as a technician with definite skills. Identify these skills and group them in appropriate classifications so that you learn to talk and write about them in these categories. Being a technician is not being someone less than you have prepared yourself to be in a career. It is understanding the world in which you live and will eventually work to such a degree that you can articulate your skill base and the attending skills you have honed. This is reflective of your marketing skills. See appendix H for a list of the skills you will exhibit if you follow the directives in this book. Believe in yourself and then you can sell yourself.

Chapter 11 Challenges

Technological

1. Chart how useful the popular culture has been in changing the workplace. Use graphics or create a chart.
2. List the traditional bachelor's degrees and in a parallel column list technical terms for describing what these degree earners are prepared to do.

3. Interview people currently doing what you want to do professionally and listen to their assessments of the workplace. After ten interviews chart and compare what you have learned. What skills have they revealed in your discussions?
4. Develop a chart that shows your own educational plans for the next ten years.
5. Develop a technical means of monitoring change and movement in your career field. What will you investigate? How will you measure what you discover?

Traditional

1. What distinguishes an entrepreneur from an intrapreneur?
2. Do you think there is such a thing as job security? If yes, why? If no, what are you going to do about remaining gainfully employed in your career?
3. Check the succession chart for your organization and identify how high you think you can go in the company before you need to look for other employment. How will you prepare yourself to recognize that moment? What will you do then?
4. Think critically about new options in your career field. Identify what this analysis could mean for you if you did it on a regular basis.
5. Think creatively about new options to keep you in the career of your choice or catapult you into another field. What could this thinking do for you? Are you prepared for the consequences? How could you become prepared?

Vocabulary

Create a dialogue, using the list of words, and describe how or in what manner you could be called a technician. The scene is a decision maker's office, and the situation is a job interview.

Better Business Bureau	dream job	professional associations
business associations	entrepreneurship	research
business breakfasts	goals	résumé
business profile	hardware	SBA
campaign	human resources management	SCORE
contemporary jobs	Internet	software
continuous job search	intrapreneurship	spreadsheet software
creative thinking	job search	strategy
critical thinking	job security	technician
cyberspace	marketplace	translator
desktop publisher	objectives	workplace
	power lunches	

Chapter 12

ENTREPRENEURSHIP

LEARNING OBJECTIVES

After you study this chapter, you should be able to

- Define and distinguish between an entrepreneur and an intrepreneur.
- Measure yourself as a potential entrepreneur.
- Know where to get good help, advice, and general business assistance to become a business owner.
- Describe the qualifications for contacting or becoming a good consultant.
- Practice ethically in the field of your choice.

- Distinguish clearly between business ownership and having a franchise.
- Describe a five-year process of beginning and developing a successful business.
- Know what kind of business owner you want to be. Or discover that you do not want to own a business.
- Identify the successful step to being a business owner.
- Know a little about the function of SCORE.
- Recognize the federal government's role in assisting you through the SBA.

LEARNING PROCESSES / SKILLS

ENTREPRENEURIAL CHARACTERISTICS

Risk Taker
Creative
Conceptualizer
Problem-Solver
Leadership
Charismatic

BUSINESS OWNERS' HELP

SBA
SCORE
Business Owners
Banks
Annual Reports
InfoTrac
ProQuest
Internet

CONSULTANT

Business Knowledge
Product/Service Expertise
Good Reputation

BUSINESS TYPES TO BUY

Successful Small Business
Business Franchise
Start Your Own Business

READINESS

Should Not Be a Question
Discernment
Good Judgment

Entrepreneurs are individuals who organize, operate, and are especially willing to risk the day-to-day ventures of new businesses. These people are frequently leaders with what seems like unlimited energy. They are often at the forefront of speculative enterprises. They risk the hazards of failure in pursuit of what is new or coming in the future. Often they are engaging people like Bill Gates, Steve Jobs, Walt Disney, and Don Hewlett; sometimes they are reclusive people like Howard Hughes and others. Their personalities come in all different dimensions, but the one thing they have in common is their willingness to risk complete failure in pursuit of a dream or idea.

Are you an entrepreneur in waiting? If you are waiting, you are probably not an entrepreneur. These individuals are often in a hurry to achieve their ideas or dreams and have already begun to work toward them. They do not wait to be assisted or evaluated but simply begin.

However, you might have an idea that will make the world a better place and want to see whether you can put it into play. Usually these ideas and dreams are about developing or designing something that does not now exist but would be a great help if it did exist. On the next page is a quick inventory you might take to evaluate yourself in light of entrepreneurship.

◼ *ENTREPRENEUR*

Deciding whether you are an entrepreneur requires self-knowledge and some hard work analyzing small businesses for yourself. Working in a small business will give you firsthand experience of all the things that can go wrong in a small business, as well as some of the challenges that face an entrepreneur.

If you have had the advantage of parents or relatives owning businesses, you will note how invaluable they consider the experience. If possible, try to get a part-time job in a family-owned business, a sole proprietorship, or a small partnership while you are going to school. Then you will be in a position to observe firsthand how a business is operated.

Entrepreneurs are significantly different people. They usually think of new and different ways of doing things, as well as new and different things to do. Creativity, innovation, and a strong sense of commitment generally mark an entrepreneur's personality.

ENTREPRENEUR'S QUIZ

Consider the following points and answer *yes* or *no*.

1. When something happens to you is it because you made it happen or because of good or bad luck? _____
2. If you could choose between working for someone else for twice your present salary, would you choose to start your own business? _____
3. When a problem surfaces that everyone around you says cannot be solved, do you usually try to solve it? _____
4. As a child, did you sell lemonade, have a paper route, or other similar activity? _____
5. Do you get along well with other people? _____
6. Do your subordinates respect you and work hard for you even if they do not necessarily like you? _____
7. Do you have a close relative who owns or who has owned a business? _____
8. Have you ever worked for a small firm in which you had close contact with the owner? _____
9. Have you ever worked for a small division of a large firm in which you had close contact with the top manager or executive? _____
10. Do you have work experience in such fields as marketing, finance, and production? _____
11. Has your employer ever rejected your "better mousetrap" ideas? _____
12. Are you between the ages of 35 and 45? _____
13. Do you like to *do* things rather than *plan* things? _____
14. Have you lived in more than three cities in your life? _____
15. Have you ever been fired? _____
16. Is your spouse/family supportive of your work? _____
17. Is the product or service you want to deliver significantly different from those already in your market area? _____
18. Do you have adequate business experience for this venture? _____
19. Can you prepare a detailed and credible business plan for the first three years you are planning to be in business? _____
20. Do you readily take responsibility? _____
21. Are you ready to put in long hours? _____
22. Will you stick to it even during rough times? _____
23. Are your resources and credit more than adequate to this pursuit? _____
24. Is your health up to the tasks ahead? _____
25. Are you a good organizer? _____

Score: Add up the number of *yes* responses. _____

22–25 You have the earmarks of an entrepreneur.
18–21 Think twice before taking the plunge. You may succeed but the chances are 50/50.
12–18 Stay where you are and enjoy your pension.
0–11 Cheer up! More than 200 million Americans are not entrepreneurs.

Some test centers have far more sensitive measuring devices than the one provided in this chapter. The search and identification of the entrepreneurial spirit has been going on for some time, especially in the United States. It is important that you have the opportunity to observe an entrepreneur at work. Discover as much as you can about attitudes toward the business, clients or customers, arrangements and contracts with vendors and employees, and approaches to bankers or other lenders. All of this information will make you a more informed decision maker.

Being an entrepreneur or working for yourself has some satisfying aspects in that you have the freedom to create your job, develop your products or services, and be responsible for generating the income of the business. This also means that when you are not open you can assume that your competitors might be. A *"gone fishin'"* sign will not appear very often in your office window. For entrepreneurs, all business losses are personal losses.

The Service Corps of Retired Executives (SCORE) is an organization of about 15,000 volunteers who counsel those who want to run their own businesses. SCORE volunteers have been successful executives in their own right and are willing to share what they learned during their years in business with any beginners who may be interested in this information.

This group started in 1964 when the Small Business Administration (SBA) announced that it would recruit more than 1,100 retired executives to help people in small businesses learn what to do to increase sales, improve profits, and solve some of the basic problems businesses have. This endeavor was under the leadership of Eugene P. Foley, who was then the SBA's administrator.

SCORE counselors come from all business fields and operations. Volunteers take a ninety-day training course, and some are rejected and not certified to counsel others in business. SCORE vouches for its volunteers, who have successful business experience, are intelligent and comfortable with other people, and know how to listen. (Call SBA's toll-free number, which is located in the federal government pages of the phone book.)

SMALL-BUSINESS ADVICE

Another way to become a business owner that is less fraught with danger is to buy a business that is already up and running. This way, if you buy an already successful business, you will realize your own dreams sooner and make a profit earlier than if you start from scratch with your ideas only. Also, banks are more likely to be open to your request for money for an existing, successful business purchase than a business that is still an idea in your head.

The research for owning your own business uses a similar strategy as recommended for looking for a job. First set your focus on an industry that appeals to you. Identify the leading companies in that field. Decide what information you need and locate various opinions about the companies and the industry.

Send for information from the company: annual report, 10K report, brochures, and addresses of interest. Look up the company's rating in the proper directory for that industry. Read what others have had to say about the company. This can be found by using InfoTrac or ProQuest to search with their CD-ROM magazine and journal bases. You can also use the Internet. Most libraries will allow you free time to search the Internet and download the information to your disk or a printer when you find something you want to peruse in greater depth.

Next begin to interview people who own businesses. You will find lots of advice from these people. In addition, they will give you leads, including names of companies that are considering selling their businesses. Treat this information confidentially and then evaluate how you will use it to achieve what you want.

Consultants

The title *consultant* used to apply to individuals who were not able to get and keep jobs in their respective fields or career choices. This is no longer true. The consultant today can name the price, go to the self-selected place, do the work as negotiated, and leave to go elsewhere when the task is finished. Reputations are made on the skill and technique the individual can use in the service of someone else who is more than willing to pay for the temporary assistance. Currently *The Wall Street Journal* lists organizations looking for consultants within its marketing pages.

It can be tough going for those who are not self-motivated and organized but have goals to accomplish. The consultant must market the services and skills possessed, find appropriate clients to serve, set adequate and competitive fees for those services, organize the business by keeping records, and manage the accounting and general office procedures. (Your office may be a side of your garage, so it needs to be organized all the more.)

How will you know if you could be a consultant?

- First, decide whether consulting is right for you.
- Second, design and develop a good-looking, eye-catching brochure.
- Third, work hard to get your first client or assignment.
- Fourth, listen to the client and tackle the assignment; close when you are finished.
- Fifth, keep in touch with the client; handle things professionally if there is a problem or something did not work out right on the assignment (try to fix it or recommend someone who could fix it).
- Sixth, match your experience and your education for insight and trust factors.

Business aspects of your practice include the following:

- First, organize and manage your business carefully: money, paper trail, time, staff, legal issues, and insurance.
- Second, set fees adequately and competitively: retainers (hourly rates or flat rate for job completion); charges for your expenses incurred doing the job; consider raising your rates when the time and economy are right; have variable rates to accommodate a variety of clients; present the bill as contracted; collect your money on time.
- Third, market yourself as a consultant: build an effective network of companies you have served; design eye-catching brochures as needed and update them often; allow for subcontracting if this becomes necessary; supervise your subcontractors' work and work habits.
- Fourth, become your own best salesperson: qualify your clients before you contract with them; prepare a good proposal and a tight contract; sell immediately after your successes.
- Fifth, sell what you know.
- Sixth, use computers and technology effectively to set up your business; maintain and use a mailing list; keep good account records of revenues; prepare fresh presentations and new materials; market electronically over the Internet, on the Web, and so forth.

Whatever you do, practice ethically within your career field, manage the stress that comes with any consultancy and individual effort, and learn when and how your business can grow and prosper.

Consultants are also available for you. Get advice about which consultants will be the most helpful. Ask entrepreneurs and business owners whom they would consult about a business situation or an opportunity to sell. Advice can be expensive, so know the price before you seek it. Advice is expensive, but that does not necessarily mean it is helpful. Be sure that you have sought opinions about the usefulness of a given consultant.

Franchises

Do not be in a hurry to buy or contract for advice about purchasing or contracting to own a franchise. Franchise owners sometimes play off their company-owned stores against business owners, franchises, especially if the business owner has accidentally hit upon a good location. Or perhaps there is something special about its logistics that the home office overlooked when offering the franchise to the business owner in the first place. With many franchises, the business owner has little or no freedom about advertising, products or services available, sources of supplies, and so on. The corporate office often controls the franchise. Some franchises work out for the advantage of the business owner, but many revert back to corporate ownership sooner or later.

Get enough information, study that information, ask questions, ask questions, and ask questions until you absorb as much as you can about the positive and negative aspects of franchise ownership or individual business ownership. Do not be in a hurry to sign contracts or negotiate deals with banks or lending institutions. Know the laws of the state in which you want to operate your business and take your time.

Some key figures in American ventures include Colonel Sanders, Orville Redenbacher, Steve Jobs, Ray Kroc, and Arthur Lukowski.
Who is Arthur Lukowski? A Chicago dreamer who consulted SCORE, spent years doing research, then opened Oil Express, Inc. He currently grosses more than $60 million a year. It is possible. It has happened to others, but it is very difficult. Maybe you have the drive, determination, and patience to succeed. Good luck!

The American dream is alive and well. Many people dream about the day they will be their own bosses. There are innumerable success stories about people who have freed themselves from the corporate jungle or the sweatshop and developed their own businesses.

When you start a business from scratch you must allow about five years before you can really say you have a successful business. It will take about three years before you can count on a salary from that business, so you need some form of income to rely on until success happens. This is why many small-business owners often begin their new businesses in their spare time. When the income from your part-time business equals more than one-half the income you make from your regular employment, you are probably ready to go full time into your new business ownership.

The story for a new business covers the following:

- First year: in the red
- Second year: meet most of the bills and payroll
- Third year: able to pay all bills on time, including bank loans and payroll
- Fourth year: pay all bills on time, including bank loans and payroll; show an appropriate profit
- Fifth year: business is doing well, profits continue, moneys are reinvested in the company or become profit for the owners

You will need to understand some tax issues before you attempt to own your own business. Hire a lawyer on an hourly basis to keep you in line with the law. The state in which you operate your business has rules about who, what, where, and when businesses can be operative within its borders. Lawyers know these things if they are any good. Again, research for the best lawyer you can afford. This decision will pay for itself in the long run.

If you do not know accounting or bookkeeping, buy the software that is clearest to operate or hire an accountant or bookkeeper to keep track of your business. You need to know what skills you have and what skills you need in people you hire in order to have an effective operation. Entrepreneurs have their own skills, but this does not include every skill that would be needed to run an effective business operation. Know where the line must be drawn and hire what help you need. Know how much help you need.

■ *BUSINESS OWNERSHIP READINESS*

Are you ready for business ownership? If this is still a question in your mind then the answer is probably not at this time. There are manuals and standardized inventories you can take to assist you in making the decision about whether to take the plunge into entrepreneurship.

Getting financing to buy a successful business may be more doable for you than franchising or starting a brand-new business. When buying an existing business remember to choose one that is doing well. This is important because a change of ownership has an effect on a business similar to that which a heart attack has on a human. Many survive and improve long after the heart attack. The same is true for businesses. However, during the period of stress that new ownership brings, you need to be as careful and sensitive as possible to business operations. Slowly bring the business back to full health.

Buying a business that is a "bargain" often results in buying a bad business or one that is sick or maybe even dying. This business will also suffer a heart attack with new ownership and often will not survive no matter how skilled you may be. Frequently the business cannot survive being in poor health and suffering the heart attack of new ownership at the same time. Some people are able to bring a business back to life, but these are exceptions to the rule.

When you buy an existing business in good financial health, take a look at the business side of the operation. Is this where you want to spend your time and energies? Suppose that you are a photographer and think you would like to buy a photography business. This could turn into a disaster if you are more interested in the photography than in the operations side of the business. You must be interested primarily in running a business, or you will see your dreams evaporate. Going into business for yourself is risky and exciting. Move cautiously and carefully if you decide to own your own business.

Steps to Being Successful in Owning Your Own Business

1. Learn as much as you can about the business you want to buy. This means knowledge about the products and services you intend to deliver. You need this business know-how to begin.
2. Build a business plan for at least one year and preferably three years indicating profit margins and personnel needs.
3. This enterprise will take more money than you have budgeted; count on it. Even when you follow professional advice and counsel, it will cost more than expected.
4. Study your competition carefully. Their established efforts are way ahead of you in the marketplace.
5. "Location, location, location" is your theme song, your bedtime and wake-up tune. Never forget it.
6. What image do you want to portray? This will be revealed in your products and services, your packaging and pricing, the development of your ads, personnel, the way they and you

treat customers, the decor of your establishment, and the delivery vehicles; everything that carries your business name reveals your business image.

7. Keep complete and accurate records for tax purposes, for the bank, and for your own information and business guidance.
8. Hire good and experienced workers, train them to serve the customer in your way of doing things, listen to their suggestions, and work with them rather than over them. They are making you money.
9. Hire excellent advisers, lawyers, accountants, bankers, insurers, managers, and promoters. You cannot do this all alone.
10. Learn what, where, and when to buy what you need because your promotional materials describe you and your business.

Chapter 12 Challenges

Technological

1. Take the quiz on page 125. Record your answers on a disk and see how you do.
2. Contact the SBA for information on SCORE. Chart the information and see whether you change your mind about becoming an entrepreneur.
3. Outline the questions you would have about buying your own business. Consider starting a brand-new one, contracting for a franchise, buying an existing and profitable business, or opening a consultancy.
4. What characteristics do you have that you could chart over and against the characteristics an entrepreneur or individual business owner would need? Show your chart to a business owner and see what remarks, ideas, and support you might get for following your dream.
5. Inform several of your friends, who also have business ownership as their goal, about your charts from the fourth challenge and your questions from the third challenge. Invite them to a session where you can all exchange ideas and leads to prepare yourselves more realistically for this option.

Traditional

1. Look up four entrepreneurs in your town and record their characteristics as you observe them. Compare and contrast the four. What insight can you glean from this comparison?
2. Read the literature and summarize your research in an essay that describes what it takes to be ready for business ownership of any dimension.
3. Take the word *entrepreneur* and begin to develop some ideas: first, recall and separate facts from concepts; second, define the terms you are using; third, organize your facts and ideas in some useful pattern or design; and fourth, show some relationship between and among your ideas about *entrepreneur*.
4. Take your ideas from the fourth technological challenge and organize a small group of your classmates who may or may not be interested in entrepreneurship for themselves. Ask them to identify where your ideas are the most clearly stated, where they have continuity within the topic, and where you are vague or ambiguous. Take that feedback and restate your purpose and goals. Are they clearer to you?

5. Make a list of the various phrases and vocabulary you hear on TV or radio or read in a journal, newspaper, magazine, or billboard. Record these in your notebook. Do this every time people suggest better ways of saying things or thinking about things that entrepreneurs address daily. Soon you will have an excellent vocabulary to talk about what you want to do and marvelous phrases to use in describing your dreams. The clearer you are, the more people will help you. Remember that many of them do not want to risk being business owners.

Vocabulary

Cluster those words that are related to entrepreneurship and show the relationship.

American dream	InfoTrac	SBA
annual report	negotiate	SCORE
business ownership	partnership	self-knowledge
CD-ROM	ProQuest	small business
consultant	readiness	sole proprietorship
entrepreneur	salary	10K report
franchise		

Chapter 13

JOB SECURITY

LEARNING OBJECTIVES

After you study this chapter, you should be able to
- Grasp and comprehend what job security is and is not in the 21st century.
- Distinguish between the definitions of full-time and part-time but permanent jobs.
- Differentiate between permanent and temporary employment.
- Comprehend the historical reasons for the initial concept of job security and its continuing development from 1850 to the present.
- Suggest some ideas that would parallel the work situations and employment possibilities in the 21st century.
- Accept that you are your own job security.
- Keep yourself up to date for continued employment in the 21st century.
- Think carefully about your future in your chosen field.
- Research meticulously before making decisions about job or career change in the 21st century.

LEARNING PROCESSES / SKILLS

JOB SECURITY

History
Current Market
Future Needs

WORKERS

Part Time
Full Time
Permanent
Temporary
Consultant

HISTORY

Industrial Revolution
Immigration to the United States

Ghettos
Depression
Collapse of Major U.S. Industries
Farm Commercialization
Changes in Technology
Labor Unions
Legislation

PERSONAL JOB SECURITY

Education
Skills
Experience
Consultant in Career
Temporary Appointments
Keep Eyes and Ears Open

What is job security? Who has it? Where are the businesses that provide it? How can you get some? These are all questions in an age of such change and economic unrest, in the United States and around the globe. Today's marketplace is ravenous for talent, skill, education, and experience. There are not many employers looking to maintain the *status quo* in their operations.

To stay on track is to be run over by competitors, technology, an educated workforce, and experienced talent.

■ *JOBS*

The concept of a permanent job in any organization is an anomaly today. The work of the immediate present is what most companies are monitoring carefully. The bottom line is more the quarter report than the annual report and not five- or ten-year analyses of the past or projection into the future. Who would have thought that AT&T, considered to be one of the most stable companies in the business world, would continue to lay off workers by the thousands year after year?

Numerous businesses today are set up to provide other businesses with qualified temporary workers. The workers come with a variety of degrees, experiences, backgrounds, and technical knowledge. Temporary agencies no longer provide only secretaries and bookkeepers to offices and accounting departments. Today the status of temporary worker stretches into the executive wings of organizations. Some executives are hired temporarily to complete certain tasks. When the tasks are completed the executives move on to other companies to perform similar services.

■ *TEMPORARY WORKERS*

People who work for temporary-placement agencies usually enjoy the variety of their work and the challenge of always working in new places. They are highly skilled workers and efficiently manage their time and work spaces. In the past they often were underpaid and received no benefits packages, significant since benefits are usually 25 to 30 percent of one's compensation within a company. Eventually temporary agencies began offering benefits packages to their workers.

This may sound like a rather forbidding way to work for more traditional employees who have worked long hours, had wages and benefits, and stayed with the same company over a long time, in some cases until retirement. Temporary workers were seen as people with limited skill but nonetheless useful to a given business need. Often they were part-time workers, who may or may not have fit into the company culture. It did not matter much since they would soon return to the placement agency; the company would then have its employee back in place.

Temporary agencies test potential workers before they are added to the agency's workforce. These workers must obey rules regarding availability, appearance, interaction with the company that has contracted for their services, the contractual agreements they have with the temporary agency, and the general decorum expected of a professional businessperson.

Today temporary agencies can contract secretarial services, nursing, accounting and bookkeeping functions, word processing, spreadsheet capabilities, electronics repair, and maintenance. They also find executive workers for organization and planning, supervision, marketing, and management at various levels. Almost any full-time worker in a "permanent" position can probably be replaced through contracts with a temporary agency.

Historical Sidebar

Historically we can see where the *job* concept came into being. Before the industrial revolution and all the changes it introduced into societies, people worked in their own homes, were artisans in their communities, or had other work for which they were compensated with bartering or money.

During the industrial revolution men left their homes and hired themselves into the service of the local manufacturing plants in nearby towns or cities. They brought home money, which was then spent for food, clothing, and shelter. Instead of making their own clothes or shoes, people started to specialize in various trades. They bought what was needed for the family from others in the region.

At the end of the 19th century and the beginning of the 20th, a vast panoply of immigrants came from Europe and the Orient to the United States to find work, money, political and religious freedom, and satisfaction of their ambitions. However, only a few found satisfying work, made good money, and became pillars of their communities. Others lived in hovels, lean-tos, or with relatives, forming ghettos and slums in the United States. They were more united in their misery than in their success.

Although these immigrants were in the United States for political and religious freedom more than financial freedom, they soon found ways to help succeeding generations get ahead. The parents of each new family hoped they would be able to pass on more wealth, values, and independence than they had experienced. Making life better for the next generation was an important goal in creating richer and freer lives for themselves.

These communities and ghettoes dot the major cities even today. Initially, people acted as though they were all one big family. Any neighborhood individual's personal success was

(continued)

Historical Sidebar

a mark of victory for the whole community. Groups of immigrants built lives together where they lived, often retaining the language of their mother countries.

Education became an issue because it was mandatory for all children of certain ages to attend school in the United States. The conflict between what the children were learning in school and what the family practiced at home was often a source of family problems, ending with members leaving home and family ties being broken. This scattered the family members all over the country, in turn enriching the nation. The diversity was a challenge for people. The family unit suffered tremendously and still does today.

Getting a job, keeping a job, doing the job, being compensated for the job, and moving up on the job are all ideas that sprang from this industrial age when people became part of the gigantic machinery that spewed its garbage into the air, dumped its wastes wherever it could, and polluted the lungs of its workers and their children. Nevertheless it was considered to be a success because people were achieving some independence. They were able to improve their living conditions as their salaries increased and their benefits packages grew. It is easy to see why the job became so important in the growing economy, as well as in the financial independence of workers.

The job was a symbol of success. To have a job was to be successful; to be without a job was to be demeaned and considered lazy. The worker who could not find a job was considered a failure in the eyes of the community and often by family members.

The first major trial of the industrial age occurred in the 1930s with the crash of the stock market and the major recession experienced in the United States and other industrialized countries. At this time thousands and thousands of workers were dismissed. Ground beef was 25 cents a pound but people did not have money, so they went hunting for food. Wild rabbit and duck became the fare of the poor and unemployed. Men filled the lines at soup kitchens.

We experience unemployment today but it is different than it was in the 1930s. In the 1970s we noticed the collapse of our major industries—automotive manufacture, sales, and service. Laid-off workers began traveling to the south and west to find comparable jobs to those held in the "rust belt" manufacturing plants. This caused a great migration and put a strain on the economy of these southern and western states.

In the 1980s we watched the farm communities collapse. Farm land was cheap in states where it had always been at a premium price. Wheat, corn, and beans, along with pork, beef, and chicken, cost the consumer little in comparison to what the farmer spent to produce them. Many farmers sold their land and became part of the migration to other states, mainly those in the south and west. Huge corporations bought many of these farms and now reap rich profits as they combine their assets and produce the food we need and send abroad. But the family farmer is a dying breed.

In the early 1990s the computer manufacturers started to collapse in the northeast. This sent many of those workers to the West Coast, where they were able to find jobs, but this put an additional strain on the economy of the western states. These layoffs continue to reach major technical manufacturers and suppliers of the new technology today. And still people look for jobs that they presume will be stable, secure, and almost eternal.

The test for job security has been taken and the grade is *F*. The idea of a job outside the confines of one's family, different from one's natural talent, and often suffocating of one's health, is the legacy of the industrial age. That makes the job an industrial age icon.

Job security has tested legislatures' capabilities to formulate and pass just laws regarding employment. Often the laws passed are so inadequate that workers feel they have no voice in the system. Unions have failed to provide all they promised to their workers, although approximately 7 to 8 percent of today's workers are union members.

◼ *CURRENT CONDITIONS*

People are growing weary of the care and feeding of the homeless, the jobless, and the forgotten lower echelons of our society. They are so numerous that no major city is without its homeless campers somewhere within its city limits. The homeless rely on the charity of their fellow citizens for survival needs. Many of these people once had good jobs in the industrialized cities of America but were laid off.

These are not the hoboes of previous decades. These people are your former coworkers. Their families are your friends. Their plight is universal. There are no jobs for them. The society and the technology and the work to be accomplished have moved on to cyberspace and they are not able to compete there. The new icon is the personal computer and the work space is the Internet. The tools are software and hardware in ever-growing technologies. The knowledge to function in this capacity is technical. The work can be accomplished in isolation, by one individual, or in teams of technically proficient personnel.

The work world is different, and you need to continue to be prepared to meet its new challenges, which change almost daily. You cannot be overwhelmed by the loss of the industrial age job. You cannot afford to look for and depend on something called job security because it does not exist. Your security lies within you. Your skills, education, and experience are what you have to sell from workstation to workstation. Your job search is never finished. You will always be looking for new opportunities, more challenging work to do, and ways to expand your own knowledge and skill level.

Do not look down on temporary positions that might be available. Think of yourself as an independent consultant who has a certain level of skills you will make available for a time and price. Be realistic. If you cannot find a job, you may be looking for something that does not exist at your level of expertise or something that is less than the best opportunity for you to use your skills and talents. You may be looking for a consulting position or a temporary appointment. Keep your options open.

The recommendation for chapter 13 is that you readjust your thinking about jobs. In light of history, it is only about 125 to 150 years old. You are on the cutting edge of the new frontier of workers. Think carefully, measure accurately, research incisively, and make decisions circumspectly. This is your first step into a career field of your choice. Step carefully so that you will not have to sidestep later.

Chapter 13 Challenges

Technological

1. Chart the history of the job in the context of U.S. workplaces from 1850 to 2000.
2. Create an image for the job as an icon for the industrial age.
3. Create an image of an icon for the computer age.
4. Formulate a graphic to illustrate the next phase of work stepping from the computer age into cyberspace or intergalactic endeavors. What would be the icon?
5. Illustrate with a graphic the work people in your chosen industry or profession do all day. Include in your graphic how one would use a degree in this backdrop.

Traditional

1. Define job security. Is it real?
2. Interview temporary workers about their skills. Compare their skills to yours. How are they different? How are they alike?
3. How have unions failed their members? How have they helped their members?
4. What laws have been passed since 1935 that benefit today's workers? Should some of them be repealed? Why? Why not?
5. What prepares you to enter today's marketplace in your chosen career field?

Vocabulary

Design a crossword puzzle using all the words in the list. Use concise and accurate definitions for the columns and rows.

benefits	full-time workers	permanent job
company culture	industrial age	placement agencies
compensation	industrial revolution	recession
consultant	job	temporary workers
contract	job security	unions
economy	marketplace	workforce
entrepreneur	part-time workers	work world

Chapter 14

CONTINUOUS JOB SEARCH

LEARNING OBJECTIVES

After you study this chapter, you should be able to

- Clarify what is happening before your eyes in the workplace.
- See what is possible for you given office politics.
- Project what your future will be if you stay with your current employer.
- Network with other professionals so that you have a clear picture of some reasonable options outside your job.

- Join a professional association.
- Seek reliable mentors in your current job and in your outside professional associations.
- Develop a marketing plan for yourself.
- Include options in your current workplace and in other businesses as well.
- Market yourself daily.
- Network with strangers and people you know in your career field.

LEARNING PROCESSES / SKILLS

IN-HOUSE	**BUSINESS PROFILE**
Politics	Career Focus/Objective
Mentor Selection	Skills
Succession Charts	Education
Business Policies	Experience
Business Portfolio	Civic Responsibilities

PROFESSIONAL ASSOCIATION	**SEARCH SKILLS**
Network	Constant, Careful Networking
Industry and the Economy	Informed Decision Making
Professional Field Associates	Professional Skills Demonstration
Daily Marketing Options	Sharp, Up-to-Date Credentials
Meeting New People	

A continuous job search may seem daunting. However, in today's markets and at today's rate of position and organizational changes, downsizing, and so on, every professional needs to be involved in a continuous job search. It will not be as extensive or intense as this first job search if you keep your doors, eyes, and ears open and communicate your career goals to your peers and supervisors.

■ *POLITICS AND THE IN-HOUSE JOB SEARCH*

The continuous job search includes participation in the in-house politics and job searching methods. You need to understand the economic picture in the country and in your own field. If you still hold ideas about job security free yourself of these unrealistic concepts. You also must understand the way your company policies dictate how promotions or lateral moves to other departments are accomplished.

Develop and design daily marketing tools to assist you in keeping the world at your fingertips. Maintain constant networking activities with other professionals in your field or in another field you wish to enter. Update your business portfolio on a monthly or bimonthly basis. Expand your professional membership activities to include more professional involvement on your part in the associations' activities. Amplify your clear and concise decision-making skills and encourage others to do the same.

In-house politics and job searching are related. Politics is about the pursuit of power; knowing who has it, who wants it, and what they intend to do with it once gained. Job searching means you have selectively identified individuals among the human resources personnel and in your own management team who can help you move to other departments and who have a say in your promotion within the company.

To play the game of politics within an organization you must understand who your friends are. Making friends in an environment in which everyone is essentially concerned about his or her own good is quite an art. Some will say that they hate politics and do not want to get involved. Too late! Employment makes you a participant in company politics whether you are active or passive, just as your birthright as an American is to vote in elections for the people who will represent you. Some vote and others do not, but both are political decisions.

Being the best at what you know how to do and knowing why you were hired are not enough to guarantee job security because you are in an environment with other people. Some are very good at politics, enjoy its challenges, and want to participate fully in the options available. These individuals usually become very good at smooth company politics and gain access to high rungs on the company's success ladder. This is not to put a bad light on their rise up the ladder as much as it is to point out that different people have different purposes for joining companies.

Others will become the best and the brightest in whatever they do for the company. Their performances are always stellar. They are disappointed often when they feel they are not appreciated for all the work they do, while the employee previously discussed seems to get all the advantages. It is not enough to be the best and the brightest. In small firms these attributes could make you indispensable, but even that situation could become boring for you eventually.

What should an employee who wants to get ahead and is poor at the political end of things do? Observe employees who are good at politics and learn from them. Ask their advice about questions you have when you do not understand their actions or why a process worked in their favor. If you find this individual is unwilling to share that information with you, find someone else to mentor you through politics in the workplace. Do not give in to discouragement or abandon the idea of understanding office politics.

You must learn how to combine your skills, education, and experience with political awareness and tactics that are not obstructionist or absurd. It is for your own good in the company, and you have to find your own way in this area. Move carefully if politics is not your strong suit. Politics is related to style in some ways. You have to have your own personality or you will be perceived as phony. As you can see, many things are at stake other than just doing your work and going home.

In-house job searches are carried out in every company. Companies say they want to promote from within as their general policy. It is a good policy, but how do you become one of the people who are promoted? First you must know where you want to go in the company. Talk with your manager or the personnel director about a succession chart. Many companies have these readily available and usually update them quite frequently to indicate who might be in line for a promotion or what steps you would have to take to move up in the company.

Succession charts clear up a lot of the mystery, gossip, and hard feelings that result when employees do not understand how individuals received recent promotions. These charts illustrate who is in line and what it takes to get in line and are usually followed fairly well when promotions are announced. An example follows.

SUCCESSION CHART

Marion Lambent Vice President of Marketing	Allison Fremont Vice President of Production	James McDonald Vice President of Finance
Jane Lamboth 15 years with company M.S. Marketing	Bill Mathews Foreman 6 years with company Technician certificate	Mary Ann Finch 2 years in accounting M.A. Accounting, C.P.A.
Susan French (New) Top Sales in Field B.S. Marketing	Frank Patterson (New) Supervisor First year with company B.S. Management	Ellen McDonald 2 years as bookkeeper B.S. Accounting, C.P.A.
Ben Lothman Sales Manager B.S. Management	Alan Lenier Special Projects Manager 10 years with company	John Decker (New) 1/2 year in department B.S. Accounting, C.P.A.

Managers in your department and in human resources need to know you want to advance in the company. If you are sure you want to transfer to a specific department, its manager should also know you would like to work there. Pay attention to the way people receive the news that you would like to improve yourself within the company. Follow the rules and submit whatever paperwork is expected. If you do not understand some process or request, ask your immediate supervisor to assist you, if that individual supports your move to better positions.

JOB SEARCH ENVIRONMENT

The state of the economy will have a lot to do with whether you move within your company or consider a move outside the company to improve your standing in the profession. Know the economic issues in your field. Study how the effect of the national economy is felt within your profession. Ask others for their opinions about the economic aspects of the national situation and your particular professional field. Do not neglect regional issues in your investigation. Some people miss what is right under their noses while searching national concerns. It is all one big picture. Keep it in perspective.

Job security is nonexistent. The only security is you and your accumulated skills, education, and experience. Keep learning and volunteer to take on difficult and complex assignments. Be careful not to overload yourself with so much work that you cannot do your regular job. That comes first in the eyes of your manager. The extra volunteering is appreciated only if your regular assignments are accomplished on time and within prescribed guidelines. Review chapter 13 if you still believe there is such a thing as job security.

DAILY NETWORKING

Marketing is a wonderful and strange animal in the business world. It can make or break a newcomer. Learn the ways of marketers and think about how those principles might be applied to selling your own skills in the public marketplace. Marketers research carefully. They promote their products or ideas often and everywhere. They are tireless in campaigns so that everyone will know what they are selling. They intrigue the buyer, making him or her inquisitive about the product or service available. The price is always right.

You need marketers' brand of confidence to promote yourself in your chosen profession. Some individuals are more reserved about announcing what they can do for others and seem to have difficulty getting the message to the prospective buyers. Others are noisy and brash in their approach and manage to annoy the buyer, who becomes disinterested. Somewhere in the middle of that continuum is where creative and innovative marketing will sell your skills, education, and experience. Find it and sell everyday. Review the marketing principles in chapters 8, 9, and 10 to refresh your memory.

Networking is the constant tool of the progressive, assertive professional in any field. Get to know who is in your profession by inviting businesspeople to lunch or to association meetings. Offer to meet them there and sit with them. Assure them that you want their counsel about something specific. Behaving well in a networking situation will serve you to great advantage. If you know someone who works a crowded room with enthusiasm and success, observe what he or she does. See how people react to the person.

Some responses are constant. If you smile at people, they will smile at you. If you remember people's names it makes them feel important and significant at the meeting. When learning individuals' names for the first time, be sure you talk with them long enough to remember their names and recognize them the next time you meet. This is a developed skill.

Introduce yourself by your given name alone. Tack some comment to that name that would be memorable to the listener. For example, "My name is Portia. My mother named me after a Shakespearean player she liked." Before you go to your family name, make sure you have correctly heard the listener's first name and have used it in conversation.

Then give some way to remember how to spell, pronounce, or recognize your family name, which will help others recall it. For example, "My family name is Haight; it is not spelled like hate but it rhymes with late." Be sure that you know the other person's last name and can spell and pronounce it correctly. Some additional memory helpers would be to make a comment, intellectual, comedic, inspirational, or outstanding, so the listener again has something to remember about you as well as your name.

If a person has not said much about himself or herself to help you remember, ask the person a question that is not intrusive and react to it or say something amusing about it so that you will remember. Make the effort because you have the opportunity to network with people everywhere you go during the course of a day or night. Learning how to use and remember individuals' names makes you memorable because so few people do so.

You are much more memorable than your printed business cards. Only give someone a business card if he or she asks for it. If you receive a card, mark the back with some notation to remind you of the person so that you remember him or her when you file the card or call this person for lunch. Building a supportive network takes work and practice. Do not let that skill wane just because you currently have a job. Keep practicing this skill; you will be grateful for what it provides you in your profession.

PROFESSIONAL BUSINESS PROFILE

When you are settled into your new position, set up a schedule for yourself to analyze your work and learn to select the new skills you are learning, the preexisting skills you are using, and the future skills you hope to learn because of the demands of this new job. On a monthly or bimonthly basis go over your contribution to your field and to your company and enumerate the many skills you are continually using for their benefit.

Call this update your professional business profile and bring an updated version when you have your reviews. Ask your supervisor to file it with your personnel papers. Tell him or her that this is the way you keep track of what you are contributing to your employer and what new skills you are developing in your job. When others ask you for an updated résumé, reply that you have a business profile you could allow them to peruse. This way you are not caught by someone who may call your boss and inquire whether these skills and education credentials are accurate. Your boss has already read the business profile and so is not threatened or worried that you are doing a job search on the side. (See appendix I for a model.)

PROFESSIONAL MEMBERSHIPS

Keep your professional memberships alive. Participate in the activities planned for members. Volunteer to assist with some of the events or to be on a committee that appeals to you. If you want exposure and promotion possibilities, volunteer for the membership or finance committee. Everyone knows these officers and the activities of these two committees are on the agenda for almost every business meeting. Keep these contacts warm and alive. They will serve you well in your profession and the association.

Chapter 14 has introduced several style issues that the job search needs to reflect and the searcher must develop. Picking up on the politics of the office or situation at hand in a company provides a certain presence. Job searching within the company for advancement requires bearing and grace. Job security is gone as an issue or a hope. Add élan to your approach of daily improvements on your self-marketing techniques; it makes you an interesting person to know.

Networking and remembering people's names are a real mark of style that people like; others may begin to expect you to remember them. Your business portfolio should be all about you and how you are becoming a better and better professional while you work for the company that currently is supervising your growth and development. Professional membership in associations gives a certain edge to your professionalism. It says something about your interest in the profession and your readiness to be involved in it aside from your daily job.

People like to be around confidence and graciousness. It makes them feel better just to be there. Think about these style issues and how they will be improved and developed as you grow into a more vibrant professional in your field.

Chapter 14 Challenges

Technological

1. If a succession chart does not exist in your company, try to develop one by yourself and see how accurate it is over two years.
2. Use the Internet to keep tabs on your profession locally, regionally, nationally, and internationally.
3. Chart your own security against what you think job security is or what was called job security twenty-five years ago.
4. Research marketing techniques and keep a chart of new methods, old methods that still work, and some combinations of both. Try new marketing techniques and see what you can generate for yourself.
5. Update and file your professional business portfolio at work and on your data disk.
6. Run for an office in your professional association and make a name for yourself in your chosen field.

Traditional

1. List the problems you have had with in-house politics.
2. Generate some different behaviors and predict how your problems could get worse or better with the new behavior.
3. Compare the results with someone who knows you in the work situation and see whether he or she agrees with your assessment.
4. Why is professional networking so important after you have found your position?

Vocabulary

Develop an expository essay to explain the interconnectedness of these vocabulary words in a business context.

business cards	human resources	politics
business portfolio	in-house politics	professional
continuous	job search	promotion
dream position	job security	research
economy	marketing tools	self-marketing
environment	networking	succession charts

Appendix A

BIBLIOGRAPHY OF PRINT MEDIA

ANDERSON, RICHARD. *Getting Ahead: Career Skills That Work for Everyone.* New York: McGraw-Hill, 1995. This text is aimed at the individual job searching within the confines of career development. The topics of business and interpersonal communication are aligned with business success.

BABER, ANNE, et al. *How to Fireproof Your Career: Survival Strategies for Volatile Times.* Berkeley, Calif.: Berkeley Publishing Group, 1995. Book is heavy on job security, which Breidenbach disagrees with completely. It is another view to consider while looking for opportunities. Overall focus is career development and vocational guidance rather than actual job search techniques.

BEILKE, INES TORRES. *Career Motivation and Self-Concept: Get Your Life on Track.* Dubuque, Iowa: Kendall Hunt/Wm. C. Brown, 1995. An interesting book of exercises to assist the searcher to become more self-actualized in the search process and personal career development.

BOLLES, RICHARD NELSON. *The 1997 What Color Is Your Parachute?* Berkeley, Calif.: Ten Speed Press, 1997. This is a perennial best-seller in the job hunting business. It has not changed much, but the career-resource pages have been updated. It is a cheerful selection of exercises sprinkled with some pep talks that usually make the user feel more confident about the job search process. It does not work for everyone and may be a real stumbling block for some.

BROMSON, ROBERT. *What Your Boss Doesn't Tell You Until It's Too Late: How to Correct Your Behavior.* New York: Fireside/Simon & Schuster Trade, 1996. Text is heavy on behavioral approaches to vocational guidance, self-evaluation techniques, some interpersonal skills needed in developing good career sense, and some basic career-development suggestions.

BURKE, ANNA MAE WALS. *How to Choose a Career Now That You Are All Grown Up.* Lanham, Md.: National Book Network, 1996. Aimed at the beginning career searcher with emphasis on the theoretical aspects of vocational guidance, career development, and self-realization understanding. Career changes are discussed, along with some tips on basic job hunting skills.

CAMPBELL, SUSAN. *From Chaos to Confidence: Survival Strategies for the New Workplace.* New York: Simon & Schuster, 1995. Long-term considerations about one's own career development, a look at the possibility of organizational change and how it affects job security, some explorations into job satisfaction, and some basic vocational guidance.

CORBIN, BILL, AND SHELBI WRIGHT. *The Edge Résumé and Job Search Strategy.* Cincinnati: Writer's Digest Books/F&W Publishers, 1995. Officially recommended text of the Professional Association of Résumé Writers. Contains full-color sample résumés and illustrates how one could stand out in a crowd of equals. Suggestions for finding opportunities and conducting aggressive campaigns are supplemented with good follow-up techniques. The book pushes the candidate to consider electronic job search techniques for the contemporary business world markets.

CROWTHER, KARMEN N. T. *Researching Your Way to a Good Job.* New York: John Wiley & Sons, 1996. Written by a librarian, this book helps the searcher understand the importance of doing research intelligently for job hunting. The best contribution is telling new candidates for professional jobs how to identify the best companies in their fields and know what information is important and why it is the key to intelligent research for a job search.

DENT, HARRY S., *Your Comprehensive Guide to Surviving and Prospecting.* Westport, Conn.: Hyperion Press, 1996. A theoretical text that analyzes organizational change and its effects on employees; the insight into manpower planning, although rather antiquated information, is well developed. The aforementioned and the effect of automation on the American labor force are under the umbrella of career-development considerations. A new look at old concepts.

ENGLEMAN, LINDA J. *Interacting with the Internet.* Burr Ridge, Ill.: Irwin/Times Mirror Higher Education Group, 1996. This text is totally devoted to helping individuals who want to search for their next professional opportunities on the Internet. The language is clear, the process is outlined carefully, and the explanations are very understandable. Everyone who is looking for a job needs this book and Internet access.

FARR, J. MICHAEL. *The Very Quick Job Search: Get a Better Job in Half the Time.* Indianapolis: Jist Works, 1995. Although not recommended by Breidenbach, this tome would be helpful for the American in a hurry. It covers mainly job hunting techniques in the United States.

FERRIS, DONNA. *The Practical Job Search Guide: Your Action Plan for Finding the Right Job.* Berkeley, Calif.: Ten Speed Press, 1996. A basic job hunting book adapted to the fast-moving market and global possibilities that searchers need to consider; a good handbook with contemporary advice and counsel. May give Richard Bolles's text some competition.

GALLO, GUY. *Take Word for Windows to the Edge.* New York: Ziff-Davis Press, 1996. This text explains macros, styles, and templates in the context of Win-Word's overall design. The fundamentals are in plain English and give hope to the uninitiated in word processing and computer wizardry. The book comes with a disk with macros, ready to run templates for résumés, and so forth.

GILSTER, PAUL. *The Internet Navigator.* New York: John Wiley & Sons, 1996. Second edition provides a comprehensive guide to the Internet, helps the searcher find a service provider, teaches how to use e-mail capability while searching, and more about how to search for a job on the Internet.

GLOSSBRENNER, ALFRED, AND EMILY GLOSSBRENNER. *Finding a Job on the Internet.* New York: McGraw-Hill, 1995. A quick study of Internet basics, enough to get started for those who have access to the Internet and an account with an on-line service. The second part is about how to do basic research on the Internet. The final part is about résumés and submitting them to the Internet. Savvy book for savvy job searchers.

GODFREY, JOLINE (ed.). *No More Frogs to Kiss: 99 Ways to Give Economic Power to Girls.* New York: HarperCollins, 1995. Contains vocational guidance for women, advice about the workforce, some theory about professional socialization, basic career-development counsel for young women, and some minor advice about basic finance.

GONYEA, JAMES C. *The On-Line Job Search Companion.* New York: McGraw-Hill, 1995. Help for the searcher who wants to use the Internet to advantage. Heavy accent on Internet use, directions for capitalizing on the network opportunities for job hunting, and good advice and counsel about the necessity of searching on the Internet as opposed to the tried-and-true methods of yesterday. America Online has provided a disk with each book, but you are under no obligation to use that service.

GORMAN, CHINA (ed.). *Executive Résumés That Work: Top Shelf Résumés and Cover Letters.* New York: Harcourt Brace Jovanovich, 1996. Executive-style résumés that may or may not apply to the recent college graduate given the number of people going back to get degrees after they have achieved several positions and promotions and been in the business world a bit. These executive approaches may be more to readers' style if they are seeking higher managerial levels in their new careers.

GRAHAM, IAN S. *The HTML Source Book.* New York: John Wiley & Sons, 1996. If you are going to make a Web page to advertise your services over the Internet, this text will assist you greatly. It covers the HTML commands, the URL syntax, Web page design, hypertext links, custom cgi-bin programs, and more. If this sounds like Greek to you, skip it.

HAYES, KIT HARRINGTON. *Managing Career Transitions: Your Career as a Work in Progress.* Scottsdale, Ariz.: Gorsuch Scarisbrick, 1996. This theoretical text discusses and gives advice about career changes, their causes, and ways to handle the crises that develop. Continuing education is a big suggestion in this text within the general rubric of career development.

HEIM, PAT, AND S. GOLANT. *Smashing the Glass Ceiling: Tactics for Women Who Want to Win in Business.* New York: Fireside/Simon & Schuster Trade, 1995. A theoretical discussion of the role of women who wish to run the fast track in a corporate culture. The issues of women's personal communication and interpersonal relationships within business are high on the authors' priorities list when giving advice to women who want to stay in business.

HENDERSON, DAVID G. *Job Search: Marketing Your Military Experience.* Harrisburg, Penn.: Stackpole Books/Commonwealth Communications Services, 1995. Individuals who have military experience and want to incorporate it into their degree skills and preparation for the job force will find the advice timely and supportive of both their learning environments.

JANDT, FRED, AND MARY B. NEMICH. *Using the Internet in Your Job Search.* Indianapolis: Jist Works, 1995. Information about searching for jobs on the Internet. Good accent on formats to use to make the résumés stand out and "say more about you than the résumé says." Advice on basic job hunting skills along with technical insight are generously provided.

JANKOWSKI, KATHERINE. *Job Seeker's Guide to Socially Responsible Companies.* New York: Visible Ink Press/Van Nostrand Reinhold, 1996. This is a comprehensive listing of one thousand companies that are socially responsible in general, as determined by thirty-four mutual funds screening devices. These include hiring practices, benefits, and social performance.

KANCHIER, CAROLE. *Dare to Change Your Job and Your Life.* Indianapolis: Jist Works, 1995. This text takes a familiar line to correlating career changes and lifestyle considerations. The causes of career changes and advice for positive career changes are interwoven in basic career-development theory.

KENNEDY, JOYCE LAIN. *Electronic Job Search Revolution: How to Win with the New Technology.* New York: John Wiley & Sons, 1995. Kennedy has written profusely on the topic of using electronics to do job searching. This includes computer network résumés, technical innovations that the software and Internet provide the searcher, and a database computer services list of providers for job hunting that is current and relatively complete.

———. *Hook Up, Get Hired! The Internet Job Search Revolution.* New York: John Wiley & Sons, 1995. A later text by Kennedy that focuses on how to do job hunting with database research techniques and recommendations and explanations about how to do job hunting on the Internet. She is a significant electronics search adviser and enthusiast.

KISIEL, MARIE. *How to Find a Job as a Paralegal: A Step-by-Step Job Search.* St. Paul, Minn.: West Publishing, 1995.This text is for paralegals, as indicated in the title. Kisiel approaches finding a legal assistant's job with enthusiasm; while Joyce Kennedy wants the searcher to use the Internet. A little vocational guidance is thrown in, along with some insight about job hunting in the United States in the current economy.

KRAGEN, KENNETH. *Grad Life Is a Contact Sport: Ten Great Career Strategies That Work.* New York: Quill/William Morrow & Co., 1995. Catchy title for a book about theoretical career-development concepts, searching problems for American candidates at home, and some vocational guidance.

KRANNICH, RON, *Dynamite Tele-Search: 101 Techniques and Tips for Getting Job Leads.* Inglewood, Calif.: Impact Publications, 1995. Good book of tips for job searching with techniques for how to use the telephone to advantage. Few people hone in on this vital tool, which frequently removes a candidate from consideration. He also discusses the use of social contacts and building networks to assist with the job search.

———. *Job Search Letters That Get Results: 201 Great Examples.* Inglewood, Calif.: Impact Publications, 1995. If you cannot write your own résumé or letters you are in more trouble than you know. However, there are some good ideas about résumé writing and cover letter concepts that job searchers could peruse and profit from.

KREUGER, CYNTHIA. *Hit the Ground Running: Communicate Your Way to Business Success.* St. Paul, Minn.: Brighton Publications, 1995. A theoretical text that discusses business communication within the frame of career development. Organizational communication, interpersonal relations, and communication within business situations are pulled together rather well.

LANDE, NATHANIEL. *Blueprinting: Rebuilding Your Relationships and Career.* New York: HarperCollins, 1995. This is a self-help book within the confines of career-development theory. There are explanations and advice to assist searchers to self-reliance, self-realization, self-management tips, and basic self-help.

MICHELOPZZI, BETTY, et al. *Coming Alive from Nine to Five: The Career Search Handbook.* Mountain View, Calif.: Mayfield Publishing, 1996. This is a sharp text that juxtaposes the theory of vocational guidance with practical situations of job hunting. Supportive of women in many ways, although that is not the focus of the text.

MR. X. *Fired? Fight Back! The No-Nonsense Guide for the Newly Fired, Downsized.* New York: Amacom Book Division, 1995. Easy to read, rather jovial if the topic were not so serious; competent unemployment suggestions with psychological underpinnings that need addressing before searchers can have enough power to do a good job finding new employment.

NOBLE, DAVID F. *Using WordPerfect in Your Job Search* (Windows/DOS, vers. 5.0–6.1). Indianapolis: Jist Works, 1995. If you do not know how to use a word processor to develop your own résumé design, this book is helpful. It is much better than the built-in résumé makers available under a variety of titles. Also, the information is current and the advice technical without being overwhelming.

ORSBORN, CAROL. *How Would Confucius Ask for a Raise? One Hundred Enlightened Solutions.* New York: Avon Books, 1995. Interesting approach to a time-honored dilemma that is even more difficult today. Orsborn's sense of humor is most helpful as she focuses on leadership, sociology, and vocational guidance to push the candidate to consider all three in light of personal career development.

PESMAN, SANDRA. *Dr. Job's Complete Career Guide: Advice for Getting Ahead in Your Career.* Lincolnwood, Ill.: Vgm Career Horizons/NTC Publishing Group, 1995. Basic text, sound advice; covers job hunting, career development, and vocational guidance all in one.

RYAN, JERRY, AND R. RYAN. *Preparing for Career Success.* St. Paul, Minn.: West Publishing, 1995. A good combination of theory and practice for the candidate to consider how to find a job in today's economy and with today's employment dilemmas, while coaching the candidate on vocational guidance and personal career-development topics. A good mix.

SEARS, SUSAN JONES. *Building Your Career: A Guide to Your Future.* Scottsdale, Ariz.: Gorsuch Scarisbrick, 1995. This book is directed toward the college-age group, meaning those in their early to mid-twenties. It focuses on employment processes within career development and vocational guidance paradigms.

SHER, BARBARA, AND BARBARA SMITH. *I Could Do Anything If I Only Knew What It Was.* New York: Dell Trade Paperbacks, 1996. Frivolous title, but good strategic suggestions for grappling with the psychological demons of indecision and apathy when going through a career search. The authors take aim at the internal conflicts that bury our desires. But the book is not pie-in-the-sky; it is very down to earth and conscious of the economic conditions and current job markets.

STEVENS, PAUL. *How to Network and Select a Mentor.* Searcy, Ark.: Resource Publications, 1995. After the job is secured or in some cases while the search is continuing, job hunters need someone to take an interest in their success and give advice about all manner of things from dress and attitude to English usage and sociability. It is a good follow-up to a great job hunting venture for the job of your dreams.

STEVENSON, OLLIE. *Great Answers to the Toughest Job Search Problems.* Hawthorne, N.J.: Career Press, 1995. This book will be helpful to anyone who is too old, too young, too inexperienced, too experienced, a female, a minority, a physically challenged person, or otherwise blocked from landing the desired job because of prejudice.

WEINBERG, JANICE. *How to Win the Job You Really Want.* New York: Henry Holt & Co., 1995. Contemporary advice and counsel about job searching, being focused on what you want, and designing your approach to go in that direction only. Good advice.

WHITE, KATE. *Why Good Girls Don't Get Ahead but Gutsy Girls Do: Nine Secrets Every Girl Should Know.* New York: Time/Warner Books, 1995. A certain rudeness and sexism in the title, but it covers current employment topics such as business issues and the role of women in business. No one would dare say that women do not belong in business, but the daily practices of business often reflect that attitude. Case studies are interesting and may give some women hope and help.

YATE, MARTIN JOHN. *Beat the Odds: Career Buoyancy Tactics for Today's Turbulent Job Market.* New York: Ballantine Books/Random House, 1995. Good writer, clear and precise in his distinctions, good analysis of the problems one will find in job hunting, especially when forced by circumstances or the economy to change careers.

———. *Knock 'em Dead, Résumés That Knock 'em Dead,* and *Cover Letters That Knock 'em Dead.* Holbrook, Mass.: Adams Publishing, 1995. The *Financial Times* of London calls *Knock 'em Dead* "the best book on job-hunting." These three books are among America's best-sellers on the topic. One unusual feature is a clear plan for running a mail campaign, plus 200 answers to really tough questions.

Software Programs

ELLSWORTH, JILL, AND MATTHEW ELLSWORTH. *The Internet Business Kit.* CD-ROM, 1995. Kit consists of *The Internet Business Book, Marketing on the Internet,* and a CD-ROM. Help with planning a marketing strategy, learning how to conduct market research, using e-mail, and accessing the resources on the Internet. The CD-ROM includes Web page templates, an HTML editor for Windows, Internet WebSurfer software, and other utilities. Expensive at $49.50 but still a good buy.

SPINNAKER. PFS: Résumé and Job Search Pro 2.0 C/Win/Us. Softkey International. 1996. Software package. Help in the form of software to enable job hunters to design and develop their individual résumés. Good ideas and easy-to-follow directions.

Softkey International. *Instant Résumé for* Windows. CD-ROM. 1996. This is not just a one-size-fits-all résumé writing guide. It is designed to help the searcher create polished, customized, professional résumés that are actually sophisticated sales tools to sell the candidate's unique talents and qualifications. Included are résumé templates, sample résumés, automatic formatting for layout combinations, spell checker, and "Action Word" glossary with a specially designed word-processing program. What more could you want?

ELECTRONIC RÉSUMÉ MEDIA SURVEY

Adams Job Bank. Adams News Media. 3.5 software package ($39.99)
    Features: 16,000 company profiles from coast to coast
        Database by industry, state, or position
        Create résumés and cover letters
        Browse 13,500 employer profiles
        Call 1,900 recorded job lines
        Contact 1,100 executive search firms
        Network 1,100 employment agencies
        Get advice on all aspects of job hunting
        Coordination of job search process
    Advice: Explore before you buy, because you may get this information elsewhere for free

B-Plan Business Planner. Windows environment. 3.5 software package. ($99.95)
    Features: Multipurpose planner with integrated spreadsheet
        Comprehensive fiscal analysis tool
        Business plan template
        Develop company history records
        Generate budget reports
        "Guide to Raising Capital" included
    Advice: For individuals going into business for themselves; good advice

B-Plan Personal Organizer. Windows environment. 3.5 software package. ($29.95)
    Features: Personal information manager
        Daily/weekly activities diary
        Phone directory
        Budget and financial planners
        Alarm mechanism to alert you to appointments
        World time map for local time in eleven cities
        Investment analysis
    Advice: One of many; if you are organized you will not need it; unorganized people must have it

cards NOW. vers. 2.0. DOS environment. 3.5 software package. ($29.99)

    Features: Print professional-quality business cards

        Includes paper for 250 cards

        View card on screen before you print

        Support for HP deskJet and laserJet printers

        Library of twenty-five clip images, ready to use

        Used in laptop computers on the road

    Advice: Easy to use; helpful tool

Career Design. DOS environment. 3.5 software package. ($29.97)

    Features: Personal career planning advice

        Innovative software

        Job search analyst

        Fashion career moves

    Advice: Costs less than a subscription to an employment weekly

CAREER PATH: Find the Job That's Right for YOU! On Track Media Corp. DOS environment 3.5 software package. ($39.95)

    Features: Research from U.S. Labor Department files

        Career analyzer technology

        Career information

        Personal evaluation

        Career directory

        Unique graphics

    Advice: Information available elsewhere; be sure you need the software before buying it

Create Your Dream Job. Wilson Learning. CD-ROM. DOS environment. ($69.95)

    Features: Probes psyche about your dreams

        Four sections covered are talents, passion, environment, and vision

        Explore what you value in a job: adventure, independence, or status

    Advice: Buy a book or see a counselor; poor-quality video clips and not worth the price

Easy Business Cards. Claris. DOS environment. 3.5 software package. ($29.98)

    Features: Do-it-yourself professional-looking business cards

        290 predesigned business card styles

        Designer paper for 250 cards

        Customize with your own data

        Prepare camera-ready art for a printer

    Advice: Easy, helpful; do you need it?

The Idea Engine. CyberKnight. WIN95, WIN3.1, MAC environments. 3.5 software package. ($44.99)

    Features: Advice, references, and entrepreneurial systems

        How-to information for inventors/designers

        Two thousand contacts for resources, parts, and services

        Compendium of data on entrepreneurial inventing

        Documents concepts, prints, and saves to the hard drive

    Advice: For entrepreneurs, designers, and artists

Job Source Plus. Panther Software. DOS environment. 3.5 software package. ($35.98)

    Features: Tailored lists of employers from 1,500 companies

An employment agency in a box

Mailmerge component to receive information and send résumés to companies

Twenty-five professional sample résumés and cover letters

Updated lists are free of charge until you find a job

Advice: Mailmerge component is worthwhile to consider if you do not have this feature with other software you own

Jump-Start Your Job Skills. Up Software. Windows environment. 3.5 software package. ($45.95)

Features: Create a database of skills, experience, and education

Build a powerful custom résumé

Present core abilities, attitudes, and bankable skills

Develop communication and marketing plans

Learn how to prioritize your skills

Publisher's sixty-day unconditional guarantee

Advice: You may know how to build databases already, but do not let that stand in your way; this is excellent software for job hunting preparation

Kaplan's Career Counselor. SSI. Windows/DOS environments. 3.5 software package. ($29.88)

Features: Acts as a personal adviser

Thorough interest survey

Extensive career information

Powerful search capabilities

Information on more than 12,700 careers

Matches careers to your interests

Sharpens job hunting skills

Advice: Good information, especially for new graduates who have not held professional positions and want to

PFS: Business Plan. Softkey International. Windows environment. 3.5 software package. ($49.95)

Features: Software combines text, charts, and spreadsheets

Program has visually stimulating layout for your data

Spreadsheets, charts, and text are electronically linked

Single entry automatically updates document

Ten templates, twenty-two layout choices

Advice: For those considering going into business for themselves; a good approach to a complicated process

PFS: Résumé and Job Search Pro. Spinnaker. Windows environment. 3.5 software package. ($39.95)

Features: Creative and impressive résumés and cover letters

Word processor with WYSIWYG view and editing

Automatic mailmerge

Ten professional templates

Automatic formatting

Free JobHunt, vers. 5.1

Built-in calendar

Advice: Good publisher and good product, but do you need it?

Quick & Easy: Federal Jobs Kit. Datatech. Windows environment. 3.5 software package. ($29.43)

Features: Automates process of filing for federal jobs

Fills out and manages the SF-171, OF612, and a government-format résumé

Prints all forms to any Windows printer

Data transfer among the forms and résumé

Advice: Important package if you want to work for the federal government, an excellent employer

Résumé Best. DOS environment. 3.5 software package. ($3.95)

Features: A job-landing tutorial

Covers all details in the preparation of a professional résumé

Includes preparation for interviews

Help with cover letters and thank-you letters is included

Advice: Comprehensive and the price is right

Résumé Builder. Resumix Inc. Windows environment. Resumix Internet Site 14.4 modem. ($12.95/month/3 hours + $2.50/additional hour)

Features: Builds résumés optimized by electronic scanning

Available on Resumix internet site

Can e-mail résumé in ASCII text

Advice: Sharp tool for computer- and Internet-literate searchers

Résumé for Microsoft Word. Microsoft. Windows environment. 3.5 software package. ($49.95)

Features: Fifty templates for résumés

Sample résumés

Advice: This is simply a résumé maker; some samples are poorly written

The Right Résumé, vers 1.0. Windows environment. 3.5 software package. ($3.95)

Features: Develops a single résumé data file

Creates custom-tailored, targeted résumés

Applies color to bullets to make text pronounced

Creates résumés that are truly yours

Advice: Accent is too heavy on the résumé, which is basically a tool, not the center of your search process; remember that its purpose is to get you an interview

Windows Résumé. SofSource. Windows environment. 3.5 software package. ($13.90)

Features: Attention-getting cover letters and résumé

Interviews that get results

Guides user through a job search process

Dozens of résumés, cover letters, and follow-up letters as samples

Advice: A little too glitzy as an approach but may work well for some

WinWay Résumé, vers 3.0. Winway Corp. Windows environment. CD-ROM available. 3.5 software package. ($35.99 for either version)

Features: Creates eye-catching résumés and letters

Manages contacts; prepares for interviews

CD-ROM version adds three hours of motion video and sound

An automatic writer suggests words and phrases for added punch

Uses custom borders, fonts, colors, and bullets

Explains necessity of knowing how to negotiate compensation; gives assistance with negotiations

Advice: Use of pat phrases seems deadening and phony with its basic say-nothing prose; the simplicity and thoroughness makes it an excellent tool; it is so easy that you may forget your job is to distinguish yourself from all those other job seekers

ZipKey, vers 3.0. DOS environment. 3.5 software package. ($3.95)

> Features: Run from DOS command line, memory resident
>> Displays correct city, state, and zip code for 30,000 cities
>> Automatically enters information into your databases
>> Also displays telephone area codes for 30,000 cities
>
> Advice: Good program; will replace your address and zip code book; cannot beat the price

Appendix C

JOB INFORMATION ON THE INTERNET

The Internet offers thousands and thousands of newsgroups, and new ones are being created daily. The ones listed here were chosen for their benefit to the job hunter. See Eric Braun's *The Internet Directory* for additional listings. Fawcett, 1996 vs. 2.0 (0-449'-98370-6)

Newsgroup Title	Area of expertise or content interest
ab.jobs	Jobs in Alberta, Canada
atl.jobs	Jobs in Atlanta
atl.resumes	Résumé postings in Atlanta
Austin.jobs	Jobs in Austin, Texas
aus.ads.jobs	Jobs available and wanted in Australia
aus.jobs	Second listing for Australia
ba.jobs.contract	Contract employment issues in San Francisco area
ba.jobs.misc	Job market in San Francisco Bay area
ba.job.offered	Job postings in San Francisco Bay area
balt.jobs	Job offerings in Baltimore/Washington, D.C. area
bionet.jobs	Professional biologists job discussions
biz.jobs.offered	Announcements for computer software/hardware electrical engineering jobs, mostly technical recruiting firms looking
bln.jobs	Jobs in Berlin; German language required
can.jobs	Jobs in Canada
chi.jobs	Jobs in Chicago
cle.jobs	Jobs in Cleveland
comp.sys.next.marketplace	NeXT hardware, software, and jobs
dc.jobs	Jobs in Washington, D.C., metro area
de.markt.jobs	Jobs in Germany; German language required
dk.jobs	Jobs in Denmark
dod.jobs	Department of Defense job postings
e.jobs	Jobs in New England
fl.jobs	Jobs in Florida

hepnet.jobs	Job announcements and discussions for high-energy and nuclear physics research
houston.jobs.offered	Jobs in Houston
hsv.jobs	Jobs in Hunstville, Alabama
ia.jobs	Jobs in Iowa
ie.jobs	Jobs in Ireland
il.jobs.misc	Jobs in Illinois
il.jobs.offered	Available jobs in Illinois area
il.jobs.resumes	Résumé postings in Illinois area
in.jobs	Jobs in Indiana
kw.jobs	Jobs in Canada (Kitchener & Waterloo)
la.jobs	Jobs in Los Angeles
mi.jobs	Jobs in Michigan
mi.wanted	Jobs and products wanted and offered for sale
milw.jobs	Jobs available in Milwaukee area
misc.jobs.contract	Contract labor discussions
misc.jobs.misc	Employment, workplace, and career discussions
misc.jobs.offered	Announcements of open positions
misc.jobs.offered.entry	Job listing only for entry-level positions; no discussion; positions: customer service representatives, sales representatives, and part-time jobs in high-tech companies
misc.jobs.resumes	Posting of résumés and help-wanted articles
ne.jobs	New England job openings
ont.jobs	Jobs in Ontario, Canada
ott.jobs	Jobs in Ottawa, Canada
osu.jobs	Jobs at Ohio State University
sci.research.careers	Issues relevant to careers in scientific research
sdnet.jobs	Jobs in San Diego
seattle.jobs.offered	Jobs in Seattle
slac.jobs	Job openings
stl.jobs	St. Louis job openings
su.jobs	Jobs wanted or available
swnet.jobs	Jobs in Sweden
tor.jobs	Jobs in Toronto
triangle.jobs	Jobs available in North Carolina research triangle area
tx.jobs	Jobs in Texas
ucb.jobs	Job announcements at the University of California, Berkeley
ucd.kiosk.jobs	Jobs at the University of California, Davis
uiuc.cs.jobs	Computer science job openings at the University of Illinois, Urbana-Champaign (UIUC)
uiuc.kiosk.jobs	University of Illinois, Urbana-Champaign
uiuc.jobs.offered	Jobs for people interested in UIUC
uiuc.misc.jobs	Jobs for people interested in UIUC
uk.jobs	Jobs wanted in the United Kingdom; no discussion
uk.jobs.d	Discussion of job-related issues in the United Kingdom
uk.jobs.offered	Jobs vacant in United Kingdom; no discussion
uk.jobs.wanted	Situations wanted; no discussion

umn.cs.jobs	Jobs at the University of Minnesota
umn.general.jobs	Jobs at the University of Minnesota
umn.itlab.jobs	Jobs at the University of Minnesota
us.jobs.contract	Contract positions in the United States
us.jobs.misc	Miscellaneous jobs in the United States
us.jobs.offered	Jobs offered in the United States
us.jobs.offered.entry	Entry-level positions in the United States
us.jobs.resumes	Résumé postings for positions in the United States
ut.jobs	Job openings and positions wanted at the University of Texas
utcs.jobs	Job announcements from the University of Texas for computer science specialists
vmsnet.employment	Jobs available and wanted and workplace and employment issues
za.ads.jobs	Jobs in South Africa

Appendix D

ELECTRONIC DATABASES FOR EMPLOYMENT

A Practical Guide to Finding a Job in Today's Frenzied Market. Audiocassette with strategies for successful job hunting. Contains résumé writing, references selection, recruiters, response to advertisers, and sample résumés.
(Cost: $7.00)

   Maximum Potential
   P.O. Box 24618
   Tempe, AZ 85285-4618
   Voice: (800) 809-0165
   Contact: Joanne Hawes

Academic Position Network. An on-line database accessible worldwide over the Internet. Provides announcements of academic position openings for faculty, staff, and administrative positions. Includes announcements for postdoctoral positions and graduate fellowships and assistantships.
(No cost to job searcher)

   William C. Norris Institute
   Suite 1548
   1 Appletree Square
   Bloomington, MN 55425
   Voice: (612) 853-0225
   Fax: (612) 853-0287
   E-mail: APN@EPX.CIS.UMN.EDU
   Contact: E. Rex Krueger, Ph.D., executive director

Access Atlanta. *The Atlantic Journal-Constitution*'s on-line database for job hunters to view the help-wanted ads. Accessible to Prodigy members.
(Cost: $4.95–$6.95/month)

   Atlanta Journal-Constitution
   72 Marietta Street
   Atlanta, GA 30303
   Voice: (404) 526-5151 or 526-5897
   Fax: (404) 526-5258
   Contact: David Scott, publisher, electronic information services

Access . . . FCO On-Line. Searchable database of federal job vacancies updated daily. Job hunters can search by GS series, grade, location, eligibility, agency, or a compilation of all. Access is available twenty-four hours a day, seven days a week, through modem and IBM PC.
(Cost: unlimited use $50/month; $25 setup fee; rates: $45/hour, $85/2 hours, and so on)

> Federal Research Service Inc.
> P.O. Box 1059
> Vienna, VA 22180-1059
> Voice: (800) 822-JOBS or (703) 281-0200
> Fax: (703) 281-7639
> Contact: Nancy Cox, vice president, general manager

ADCo/Advanced Concepts Services. Database of government job openings, updated daily, offered on diskettes and on electronic career guide.
(Cost: $9.95)

> ADCo/Advanced Concepts Services
> Department AC2
> P.O. Box 3821
> Lynnwood, WA 98046
> Voice: (206) 546-8665
> Fax: (206) 365-5055
> CompuServe: 76020,3062
> Contact: Nick Pearson

America Online Whale Express. Use a trial version of its script program to see if you want to spend the money to use the services. Get access to the information on disk through land mail or by downloading the trial version through AOL.
(Cost: $40)

> Tartan Software
> 143 Horstman Dr.
> Scotia, NY 12302
> Voice: (518) 372-3990
> AOL: tartan@aol.com

Broadcast Employment Weekly. A BBS hot line for job openings in radio and television stations.
(Cost: $25–$30)

> Broadcast Employment Weekly
> 1125 W. Boone Ave.
> Nampa, ID 83651-1812
> Voice: (800) 922-5627 or (208) 463-1951
> Fax: (208) 467-4097
> BBS: (208) 467-4110
> Contact: Brian Denny, president

//CAREER. Menu-driven database made up of information from *The National Business Employment Weekly.* "Talent for Hire" section updated monthly. Helpful advice articles appear often within the database regarding job searching problems and suggestions for job hunters.
(Cost: $19.95 annual fee plus $1.50/1,000 characters of information)

> Dow Jones News/Retrieval
> Dow Jones Business Information Services
> P.O. Box 300
> Princeton, NJ 08543
> Voice: (609) 520-4638
> Fax: (609) 520-4660
> Customer service: voice: (800) 522-3567; fax: (609) 520-4775

Career Net Graduate. Résumé database for new college graduates. Job hunters use disk to submit résumés, which are combined with others on a CD-ROM accessible to employers. Search is by keywords. (Cost: Less than $100 but still expensive)
> Career Net Graduate
> 643 W. Crosstown Pky.
> Kalamazoo, MI 49008
> Voice: (616) 344-3017

Career Systems Online. Free access through a modem to job listings in fields of programming, software engineering, and software development.
(No cost)
> Systems Personnel
> P.O. Box 63
> Chicopee, MA 01014
> Voice: (413) 592-4069
> Fax: (413) 592-9255
> Modem: (413) 592-9208
> Contact: Donna Frappier

Classifacts. Database of approximately 125,000 help-wanted ads from newspapers in its single database, updated weekly. Results available by first-class mail, next-day or second-day delivery, or same-day fax. (Cost: $29.95/4-week subscriptions, $4.95/each additional week)
> North American Classifacts
> 2821 South Parker Rd.
> Suite 305
> Aurora, CO 80014
> Voice: (800) 789-8974
> Contact: customer service

CompuServe Navigator. Script program that automates the time you spend, reduces connect time, and could save you billing time. Support help is available to get started.
(Cost: $50, $25 of which is a CompuServe usage credit)
> Follow steps from CompuServe's information services' opening page

Delphi D-Lite. Cuts on-line costs, does full-screen editing, and will automatically download multiple files. A good way to follow informal job postings on the newsgroups.
(Cost: $29 registration fee)
> Circular Logic
> P.O. Box 162
> Skippack, PA 19474
> Voice: (610) 584-0300
> Fax: (610) 584-1038
> Internet: Perry@Delphi.com

Direct Link. Database focused for people with disabilities. Job hunters find resources for job training and placement, occupational skills training, and vocational rehabilitation.
(No cost to disabled or their families)
> Direct Link for the Disabled Inc.
> P.O. Box 1036
> Solvang, CA 93464
> Voice: (805) 688-1603
> Fax: (805) 686-5285
> Contact: Linda Lee Harry, executive director

Electronic Job Matching. Computerized database of electronic portfolios of job hunters; more than a résumé listing. Employers can search by skills, proficiency level, industrial background, salary, education, work experience, and relocation factors if there are any. Mail your résumé with indication of positions acceptable to you to address given.
(No cost to job hunters; employers pay a fee)

> Electronic Job Matching
> 1915 North Dale Mabry Hwy.
> Suite 307
> Tampa, FL 33607
> Voice: (813) 879-4100
> Fax: (813) 870-1883
> Contact: program director

E-SPAN. Database of help-wanted ads on America Online and CompuServe, updated weekly and available through these network services.
(Cost: Charges for America Online or CompuServe membership)

> E-SPAN
> 8440 Woodfield Crossing
> Suite 170
> Indianapolis, IN 46240
> Voice: (800) 682-2901
> Contact: customer service

Euro Pages on CD-ROM. Database of 150,000 European companies by names, phone numbers, and addresses. No metering system; data are available for one unlimited usage program through select phone but can be purchased separately.
(Cost: free when purchased with select phone)

> ProPhone Inc.
> 8 Doaks Lane
> Little Harbor
> Marblehead, MA 01945-9866
> Voice: (800) 99-CD-ROM
> Contact: support service

Exec-PC BBS. World's largest BBS on-line searchable databases where companies post job openings and job hunters post résumés. New addition to BBS is concept of using floppy-disk-based résumés. Demonstrations provided for this experimental area. Modem access.
(Cost: $4/hour [local access from anywhere in the United States] to $75/year, $25/3 months)

> Exec-PC
> Elm Grove, WI 53122
> Voice: (414) 789-4200 or (800) EXECPC-1
> Modem: (414) 789-4360, 14,400 bps V.32 bis; (414) 789-4210 2400 bps; (414) 789-4500 28,800 bps
> Contact: customer service

"FIND-IT-511." An interactive telephone service. Job seekers may call to obtain information about employment positions in Georgia.
(Cost: 50¢/call)

> Info Ventures of Atlanta
> 44 Broad St., NW
> Suite 710
> Atlanta, GA 30303-9718
> Voice: (404) 222-2000
> Contact: Jennifer Easterly

Genie PC Aladdin. Off-line messaging ability saves you money.
(No Cost)
> Follow steps to download from Genic home screen menu bar; select "on-line."

IFMA Job Referral Service. Database of résumés of facility managers, searched by employers to locate appropriate candidates. Copies of résumés are then provided to employers.
(No cost to job seekers; $295 per search for employers)
> International Facility Management Association
> 1 East Greenway Plaza
> Suite 1100
> Houston, TX 77046-0194
> Voice: (713) 623-4362 or (800) 359-4362
> Fax: (713) 623-6124
> Contact: research specialist

HispanData. Database for Hispanic college-educated professionals and managers. Fortune 500 companies have access to database through HispanData. Send résumé to address.
(Cost: $25/résumé; $10/update résumé)
> HispanData
> 360 South Hope Ave.
> Suite 300-C
> Santa Barbara, CA 93105
> Voice: (805) 682-5843
> Fax: (805) 687-4546
> Contact: program manager

J. O. B. Database serving blind U.S. residents looking for employment. Other job-related services are available in addition to the BBS service called NFB Net. Services are designed to help job hunters and employers.
(No Cost)
> National Federation of the Blind
> 1800 Johnson St.
> Baltimore, MD 21230
> Voice: (410) 659-9314 or (800) 638-7518
> BBS: (410) 752-5011
> Contact: Lorraine Rovig, director

Job Bank USA. Database of 30,000+ résumés at any given time. Nationwide, comprehensive, all-purpose recruiting resource. Call and request enrollment form. Send résumé and enrollment form. You will be called to verify your qualifications by Job Bank USA. You are not referred without your permission to avoid wasting employers' time and to protect the privacy of individuals seeking new positions.
(Cost: $30 annually)
> Job Bank USA
> 1420 Spring Hill Rd.
> Suite 480
> McLean, VA 22102
> Voice: (800) 296-1USA
> Fax: (703) 847-1494

Job and Career BBS List. On-line access to searchable lists of job- and career-oriented BBSs. Full contact information and detailed description of services offered. More than 5,000 current employment ads on-line. Career and job search information, corporate and recruiter databases, and career counseling available on-line.
(No cost to Philadelphia-area résumé database; $5.00 everywhere else)

> On-line Opportunities
> P.O. Box 17
> Dowington, PA 19335
> Voice: (610) 873-2168
> BBS: (610) 873-7170
> Contact: Ward Christmas, executive director

The JobBank Hotline. Offers California Chicano News Media Association members a toll-free, twenty-four-hour hot line to access information about media job openings. Average fifty jobs per week in every media field: TV, radio, print, education, advertising, and public relations.
(Cost: free to members; $35 for journalists; $10 for students)

> The California Chicano News Media Association
> 727 W. 27th St.
> Los Angeles, CA 90007
> Voice: (213) 743-7158
> Fax: (213) 744-1809
> Contact: Al Reyes, executive director

Job Link. Hot line serving Puget Sound and Seattle, Washington areas. Searchers call in and preview the ads twenty-four hours a day, seven days a week.
(No Cost)

> *The Employment Paper*
> 209 Sixth Ave. N
> Seattle, WA 98109
> Voice: (206) 441-4545
> Fax: (206) 441-4226
> Hot Line: (206) 517-5627
> Contact: customer service

JOBBS. BBS lists thousands of national job openings, mostly high-tech and engineering. Also offers free job hunting advice for job seekers.
(No cost to job hunters)

> Alpha Systems Inc.
> 1510 Oakfield Ln.
> Roswell, GA 30075-3013
> Voice: (404) 992-8663
> Modem: (404) 992-8937
> Contact: Bill Griffin, sysop/president

JobLine. Hot line to access new job openings at public radio and TV stations nationally. Lists of jobs available twenty-four hours daily, updated weekly. Use push-button phone.
(Cost: cost of telephone call)

> The Corporation for Public Broadcasting
> 901 E St. NW
> Washington, DC 20004-2037
> Voice: (202) 879-9600
> Fax: (202) 783-1019
> JOBLINE: (202) 393-1045
> Contact: follow voice instructions

JOBTRAK. On-line database accessible to searchers and employers.
(No cost to colleges, students, and alumni/alumnae)

> JOBTRAK
> 1990 Westwood Blvd.
> Suite 260
> Los Angeles, CA 90025
> Voice: (310) 474-3377 or (800) 999-8725
> Fax: (310) 475-7912
> Contact: Ken Ramberg, CFO

Nando.Net. BBS provides employment classified ads from Raleigh, North Carolina's *The News & Observer* newspaper.
(Cost: $15–$30/month)

> *The News & Observer*
> 215 S. McDowell St.
> P.O. Box 191
> Raleigh, NC 27602
> Voice: (919) 836-2808
> Fax: (919) 836-2814
> Modem: (919) 829-3560 or (919) 558-0500
> Telnet: Merlin.NandO.net (logon as guest)
> Contact: Denise J. Jones

National Résumé Bank. Provides database for job hunters to send their résumés for review by employers.
(Cost: $40; no cost to employers to search database)

> National Résumé Bank
> 3637 Fourth St. N.
> Suite 330
> St. Petersburg, FL 33704
> Voice: (813) 896-3694
> Modem: (813) 822-7082
> Contact: NRB Headquarters

Networking Career Online. Database listing of computer-network specialist job opportunities. Used by job hunters and employers alike.
(No cost)

> Network World Inc.
> 161 Worchester Rd.
> Framingham, MA 01701
> Voice: (508) 875-6400
> Fax: (508) 820-1283
> Modem: (508) 620-1160
> Contact: William Reinstein

Resume-Link. Market-specific database of degreed professionals with experience in computer and engineering fields. Employers have access to database on a subscription basis.
(Cost: $50/year)

> Resume-Link
> 3972-C Brown Park Dr.
> Hilliard, OH 43026
> Voice: (614) 777-4000
> Fax: (614) 771-5708

U.S. Department of Commerce, Bureau of Census. Database access with a modem to current vacancies within the Census Bureau in Washington, D.C.
(No cost)

U.S. Department of Commerce
Bureau of Census, Personnel Division
Room 3124, FB 3
Washington, DC 20233
Voice: (301) 763-5780 or (800) 638-6719
TTY: (301) 763-4944
Modem: (800) 451-6128
Contact: Sandra Loew, (301) 763-5780

Appendix E

THE LAW AND YOU

Historical Legal Considerations

The Constitution of the United States

Amendments 1 and 5 within the Bill of Rights forbid discrimination based on religion, guarantee free speech, and forbid deprivation of life, liberty, and the pursuit of happiness without due process of law.

Civil Rights Acts: 1866 (13th Amendment), 1871, 1964, 1967, 1968, 1972, 1974, 1986, 1987, and 1991

In one way or another and sometimes in a summation of rights, the Constitution and its amendments guarantee freedom from discrimination based on religion, race, national origin, color, gender, age, physical or mental disabilities, and citizenship and require employers to provide accommodations for the disabled.

Constitutional Protections: Davis-Bacon, Walsh-Healy, Wagner, Unemployment Compensation, Fair Labor Standards, Labor-Management Relations, Equal Pay, Occupational Safety and Health (OSHA), Title Seven Amendment, Equal Employment Opportunity Commission (EEOC), Vietnam-Era Veteran's Readjustment, Privacy, Employee Retirement Income Security (ERISA), Minimum Wage, Pregnancy Discrimination, 1980 Sexual Harassment Guidelines, Employee Polygraph Protection, and Plant Closings

The listed legislative acts, among others on the books, provide various options for employees and in some cases employers. These laws collectively include guarantees of prevailing wages for government contractors, employees' right to organize, collective bargaining in management-labor disputes, establishment of unions, income for fired or laid-off employees, minimum wage, controlled hours, premium pay for overtime, control of the hours children may work, good-faith bargaining in disputes, outlawing of closed shops, prohibition of strikes in national emergencies, equal pay for equal work, reasonably safe workplace, affirmative action, protection of employees' pension funds, diverse national workplace, pregnancy defined as disability for benefits of disability coverage, and freedom from sexual harassment.

Executive orders and other laws pertaining only to government employees: 1962, 1965, 1974, and 1978 civil service reform

These orders and the 1978 legislative act provide assurances to government employees for the right to join unions and bargain collectively; agencies must confer with unions on policy practices and working conditions; office of Federal Contract Compliance (FCC) forbids discrimination based on race, color, gender, religion, national origin, and physical or mental disability; affirmative action required; employees can review employers' records on them to bring civil damages, if warranted; and civil service reform guaranteed a "workplace reflective of the nation's diversity."

Congressional action on behalf of employees: Family and Medical Leave Act of 1993, Gender Equity Act of 1993.

The Family and Medical Leave Act guarantees that people who must attend to medical situations in their immediate families, including themselves, must be granted the time and have the assurance that their jobs will be waiting for them at the end of the twelve weeks allotted by the legislation. Many details amplify this law, but this is its basic gist.

The Gender Equity Law of 1993 established an Office of Gender Equity, which provides money for studies and supervises and authorizes grant expenditures.

Continuing Legislation Surrounding Employment

Another minimum-wage law was passed by Congress and signed by the president in 1996. Keep current with your research about what laws exist to protect you and what those laws provide you as a citizen of and worker in the United States. There are also additional laws passed by state legislatures that need to be studied and followed by you and your potential employer. State legislation is more widespread in its coverage, more specific in its language, and often ahead of federal legislation because Congress often follows the lead of states when designing legislation.

Supreme Court decisions often push Congress to enact new legislation, as in the case of the Civil Rights Act of 1991. Congress is considering issues like further defining sexual harassment beyond the 1980 law because of recent Supreme Court decisions regarding relevant lawsuits. Affirmative action reform is a hot topic that will surely continue to be debated. Keep alert, read, listen, study, and be prepared.

PERSONALITY INVENTORY

Read each of the columns below and mark an X on the line preceding the top five words in each column that you feel best describe your personality most of the time. Proceed by supplying "I am . . ." or "I am a . . ." before most of the words.

RI	AP	IP	AS	CODE
___accomplished	___demonstrative	___tenacious	___courteous	___ 04
___satisfied	___insensitive	___opportunistic	___scattered	___14
___commanding	___generous	___dubious	___detailed	___20
___confident	___agreeable	___good natured	___forgetful	___13
___weak kneed	___listener	___unpredictable	___free	___03
___careful	___believable	___self-possessed	___seasoned	___11
___determined	___convincing	___predictable	___dreamy	___18
___diligent	___authentic	___fault finding	___energetic	___07
___calm	___reserved	___nervous	___inexact	___02
___compliant	___private	___impatient	___precise	___01
___systematic	___self-assured	___mobile	___open	___09
___moderate	___backward	___uneasy	___masterful	___05
___stable	___self-advancing	___receiver	___principled	___15
___even tempered	___delightful	___harmonious	___cold	___12
___impatient	___talkative	___teachable	___methodical	___17
___vivacious	___impetuous	___faithful	___tactful	___16
___pensive	___thoughtful	___zealous	___tense	___08
___offensive	___outgoing	___secure	___accurate	___19
___demanding	___big hearted	___attentive	___focused	___10
___circumspect	___unbelievable	___passionate	___obstinate	___06
TOTALS _____	_____	_____	_____	

Place the code form of the last column opposite and to the right of each column, covering the words of the column. Line up the horizontal lines on the code form with the horizontal lines in each column from top to bottom. Write the numbers indicated in the code column in the spaces marked. Mark only five in each column. Total each column.

PERSONALITY SKETCH CLUES

Once you have completed the personality sketch, select the column with the highest score. This column may be the one that best describes your personality most of the time. You may discover characteristics in all four areas. This is true of most people. What you are doing is discovering the predominant personality clues for greater insight into yourself. A look at the qualities and characteristics you possess naturally will help you formulate your marketing plan with more precision and accuracy.

Study the table below. Reflect on the section where you have the most characteristics. Inspect the general tendencies and examine the positive and negative aspects of your predominant qualities. You are looking for insight into yourself, your personality, and your motivations. Do not be a mystery to yourself. Be honest. This is your life.

Personality Profiles

	Attitudes	Strengths	Weaknesses	Desires
Sketch	"I am characterized by …"	"I am energized by …"	"My shortcomings are …"	"In a job I need …"
RI	Realism	Detail	Overly accurate	Concentration
	Diplomacy	Caution	Procrastinating	Precision
	Organization	Orthodoxy	Unable to delegate	Encouragement
	Politics	Rationality	Fearful of job reviews	Work guidelines
	Comprehension	Perceptiveness		Clarity

My *general* tendency is to see all sides and be intuitive. I am intolerant of differing views and reject criticism.

AP	Assurance	Problem solving	Indiscreet	Position
	Fearlessness	Decision making	Domineering	Authority
	Self-centeredness	Goal setting	Spontaneous	Prominence
	Power	Pioneer spirit	Fearful of others'	Power
	Energy	Creativity	opportunism	Open speech

My *general* tendency is to be direct and goal oriented. I seldom listen to others and often dismiss their ideas/opinions.

IP	Cheerfulness	Inspiration	Easily persuaded	Status
	Sociability	Communication	Roundabout	Accreditation
	Fluent speech	Performance	Unaware of time passing	Independence
	Impetuous	Collaboration	Fearful of losing social	Acceptance
	Sensuality	Assisting others	contacts	Speak out

My *general* tendency is to respect others and be open-minded. I am often too sensitive and defensive.

AS	Faithfulness	Concentration	Retentive	Stability
	Stability	Individualization	Convivial	Convention
	Leisure style	Cohesiveness	Assured	Assurances
	Long-suffering	Security	Fearful of losing security	Community
	Predictability	Attentiveness		Acknowledgment

My *general* tendency is to listen and have balanced reactions. I avoid conflict at all costs.

SUMMARY

This personality profile, based on your own assessment, enables you to become aware of your personality. In the attitudes column are words that describe your personality. Is the result at least 80 to 85 percent accurate about you? The strengths and weaknesses columns describe your characteristics. They are two-edged swords. Example: Decisive people who push decision making too hard can become domineering. Detail-oriented people can become overly precise. The desires column describes what kinds of things would give you job satisfaction in the workplace.

In the overall population between 15 and 20 percent are realistic introverts (RI: exacting, critical people generally), authentic power (AP: powerful, dominant people), or influential power (IP: influential and authentic people). Approximately 45 to 55 percent are accurate sensing (AS: constant and faithful people generally).

Looking at these data you want to ask yourself whether this is the way you see yourself. Is this how your friends would describe you? And what do business associates and relatives see in your personality? This examination will help you understand yourself and your readiness for certain workplaces and markets. Test your insight against the ideas and suggestions of the people in your support group for additional verification.

Source: The psychological theories underlying this instrument are based on research and findings of eminent psychological theorists and clinicians as this information has been made public over the last century. The instrument design and focus are original and of proprietary interest to the author. The ideas and research used in developing this instrument find their roots in Carl Jung's personality theories, Meyers/Briggs's theories for testing personalities, Richard Bolles's personal assessment tools, Jackson's personality characteristics scales, and Charles Hampden-Turner's brain personality theories.

Appendix G

STANDARD U.S. POST OFFICE DESIGNATIONS AND DOMAIN ADDRESSES

Speedier mail service begins with the front of the envelope:

1. Attention line always goes above the firm name.
2. The delivery address includes either the street address, the P.O. box number, rural route number, or highway contract route number
3. Include the RM (room), STE (suite), or APT (apartment) number.
4. The last line is reserved solely for the city, state, and zip code or zip code + 4 digits.

5. Always use your return address.
6. Use ST (Street), AVE (Avenue), PL (Place), DR (Drive), LN (Lane), RD (Road), CIR (Circle), and so forth.
7. Indicate whether it is N (North), E (East), W (West), or S (South), as necessary.
8. Be consistent; use only traditional abbreviations.

STATES

Alabama	AL	Kentucky	KY	North Dakota	ND
Alaska	AK	Louisiana	LA	Ohio	OH
Arizona	AZ	Maine	ME	Oklahoma	OK
Arkansas	AR	Maryland	MD	Oregon	OR
California	CA	Massachusetts	MA	Pennsylvania	PA
Colorado	CO	Michigan	MI	Puerto Rico	PR
Connecticut	CT	Minnesota	MN	Rhode Island	RI
Delaware	DE	Mississippi	MS	South Carolina	SC
District of		Missouri	MO	South Dakota	SD
Columbia	DC	Montana	MT	Tennessee	TN
Florida	FL	Nebraska	NE	Texas	TX
Georgia	GA	Nevada	NV	Utah	UT
Hawaii	HI	New Hampshire	NH	Vermont	VT
Idaho	ID	New Jersey	NJ	Virginia	VA
Illinois	IL	New Mexico	NM	Washington	WA
Indiana	IN	New York	NY	West Virginia	WV
Iowa	IA	North Carolina	NC	Wisconsin	WI
Kansas	KS			Wyoming	WY

Avenue	AVE	Expressway	EXPY	Road	RD
Boulevard	BLVD	Freeway	FWY	Square	SQ
Circle	CIR	Lane	LN	Street	ST
Court	CT	Parkway	PKY	Turnpike	TPKE

North	N	Northeast	NE	East	E
South	S	West	W	Northwest	NW
Southeast	SE			Southwest	SW

MOST COMMON TOP-LEVEL DOMAINS

.com	commercial
.edu	educational
.gov	government
.int	international
.mil	military
.net	network
.org	nonprofit organization

Example: *gopher.dartmouth.edu*

SELECTED INTERNATIONAL DOMAIN EXTENSION CODES

.au	Australia	.fr	France	.nl	Netherlands
.ca	Canada	.ie	Ireland	.no	Norway
.ch	Switzerland	.il	Israel	.nz	New Zealand
.de	Germany	.in	India	.pl	Poland
.dk	Denmark	.it	Italy	.ru	Russia
.es	Spain	.jp	Japan	.se	Sweden
.fi	Finland	.mx	Mexico	.uk	United Kingdom
		.us	United States		

Example: *preisendorfer@gold.com.de*

Appendix H

RÉSUMÉ SKILL WORDS LIST

Use these lists to refine, expand, create, develop, improve, and design a more professional looking résumé, but remember to be truthful in describing yourself and your various accomplishments. Consider describing yourself in terms of your skills rather than expecting potential employers to translate how your degrees and experience might be useful to them. Do not use a word you do not understand. Of course you are not limited to these lists. Resort to these lists after you have set your goals, identified your skills, selected your experience factors, and formulated the first draft of a résumé. Then use these lists or a thesaurus to amplify, clarify, develop, describe, and create the most attractive, eye-catching, and truthful résumé possible.

NOUNS
(A word used to name a person, place, object, idea, quality, or activity)

vendor	master_____	ability	wizard
_____smith	employee	facility	style
readiness	competence	dexterity	mode
technique	prowess	adroitness	expert
balance	energy	system	ease
deftness	posture	prospect	trend
status	communication	entrepreneur	poise
forecast	spontaneity	demeanor	vigor
bearing	high performer	appearance	mien
presence	manner	custom	look
praxis	practice	reputation	manager
prestige	station	stance	usage
attitude	agility	distinction	state
method	operative	composure	rank
readiness	work	capability	grace
agility	pursuit	study	vitality
résumé	habit	custom	urbanity
exercise	message	report	rehearsal
contact	dignity	director	usage
notoriety	foreman	officer	character
supervisor	administrator	leader	superintendent
official	guide	mentor	executive
pilot	service	favor	chief
altruism	business	trade	conscience
honor	industry	commerce	kindness
lookout	corporation	establishment	company
firm	vocation	job	enterprise
outfit	effort	duty	employment
occupation	position	purpose	task
chore	distinction	appointment	role
function	uprightness	accolade	prospect
outlook	appreciation	respect	integrity
rectitude	technician	esteem	respect
regard	expertise	craft	estimation
worker			

VERBS
(A word that expresses existence, action, or occurrence; in résumé writing you may find the past tense of these active verbs more accurate)

operate	supervise	compete	consider
encourage	able	balance	motivate
plan	affect	produce	organize
act	ease	conciliate	qualify
effect	energize	intellectualize	compose
facilitate	dignify	communicate	grace
settle	expedite	alleviate	handle
systematize	allay	evaluate	enunciate
forecast	market	deal	mitigate
assuage	characterize	entitle	function
customize	work out	pursue	trade
designate	exploit	implement	employ
exercise	beautify	embellish	actuate
use	admire	value	consider
enhance	distinguish	ennoble	esteem
regard	acclaim	extol	laud
elevate	conduct	oversee	fare
praise	purchase	administer	buy
govern	run	sequence	teach
educate	instruct	discipline	tutor
present	point	direct	aim
head	cast	level	zero in
correct	pass	follow up	trail
follow	sell	chase	rush
spark	appropriate	merchandise	vend
handle	evaluate	purchase	allocate
appoint	indicate	earmark	nominate
show	calculate	assess	denote
estimate	impose	specify	rate
assay	determine	judge	levy
review	conclude	exact	referee
gather	think	decide	infer
gauge	design	deduce	observe
develop	manage		

ADJECTIVES
(A word that answers the question what kind, how many, or which one; the word modifies the
meaning of a noun or pronoun)

skilled	serious	technical	effective
self-employed	energetic	earnest	proficient
businesslike	forceful	enterprising	no-nonsense
adept	strong	independent	peppy
vigorous	robust	powerful	ingenious
active	composed	calm	competent
qualified	productive	dexterous	instinctive
balanced	agile	graceful	political
expert	deft	conciliatory	handy
gentle	smart	alert	adroit
quick-witted	steady	intelligent	realistic
pragmatic	dynamic	high-performance	well-groomed
systematic	spontaneous	organized	quiet
dignified	artistic	practical	poised
artful	orderly	innovative	functional
methodical	uniform	tidy	complex
regular	constant	even	urbane
true	staunch	firm	stable
resolute	lively	steadfast	loyal
efficient	tasteful	driving	aesthetic
unprecedented	inventive	original	novel
bold	bright	creative	ingenious
keen	witty	sharp	sharp-witted
chic	modish	humorous	scintillating
wise	shrewd	stylish	dashing
perspicacious	amusing	frugal	astute
jocular	facetious	comical	zany
skillful	contingent	trim	shipshape
efficacious			

ADVERBS
(A word that answers the question when, where, why, in what manner, or to what extent; the word modifies the meaning of a verb, an adjective, or another adverb; often ends in -*ly*)

effectively	efficaciously	astutely	seriously
earnestly	energetically	proficiently	actively
powerfully	vitally	forcefully	genuinely
surpassingly	robustly	quickly	tastefully
instinctively	gracefully	calmly	skillfully
easily	gently	expertly	deftly
realistically	pragmatically	quick-wittedly	efficiently
adroitly	smartly	steadily	quietly
distinctly	vigorously	systematically	neatly
quickly	dynamically	spontaneously	practically
expeditiously	briskly	effortlessly	masterly
functionally	attitudinally	cleverly	competently
orderly	ethnically	complexly	intelligently
dexterously	politically	independently	briskly
artistically	artfully	handily	accidentally
inadvertently	methodically	neatly	conditionally
smoothly	fortuitously	casually	fluidly
elegantly	fluently	relatively	tranquilly
coolly	exquisitely	imperturbably	nonchalantly
placidly	evenly	prettily	boldly
presumptuously	serenely	keenly	audaciously
brightly	impudently	knowingly	fashionably
wisely	alertly		

B.S., Education/1 Year Experience/Tutoring English Usage

Dona Frank   Voice: (656) 555-4326
3278 Main Street   Office: (656) 555-6754
Dayton, Montana 00000   e-mail: BunnyFrank@000.edu

CAREER   *Elementary Education/English Tutor/Reading Readiness,* where developed skills
FOCUS: in English composition, reading comprehension, and child counseling will
             enable a school to improve its students' individual standings on national tests
             of reading and English usage; counseling the students with these deficiencies
             to improve their abilities within six to eight months.

SKILLS   *English Usage*   *Reading*   *Counseling*
PROFILE: **Sentence Structures**   **Vocabulary**   **Young Child**
             Grammar   **Comprehension**   **Development**
             Usage Skills   **Speed**   **Problem Solving**
             Story Building   **Verbal Reading**   **Guidance**
             Spelling   **Acting in Plays**   **Group Work**

EDUCATION: **B.S. (Elementary Education)** University of Southern Michigan.
                 Jackson, Michigan, *cum laude*

                 Significant Theory Courses: *Important Lab Courses:*
                 Principles of Child Development   Speech Labs
                 Education Theory (I, II, III)   Language Labs (English)
                 English Composition   Lesson Planning Lab

                 Relevant Projects:
                 Practiced Teaching
                 Developed Training Tool for Slow Readers
                 Designed Spelling Lab for Computers (senior project)

EXPERIENCE: *Teaching Assistant.* St. Michael's Episcopal Elementary School. Jackson,
                  Michigan (1997–1998)
                  Developed lesson plans under supervision of classroom teacher and
                  presented these lessons to fifth graders for an eight-week student grading
                  period.

                  Teaching Assistant. Inner-City Summer Curriculum. Jackson, Michigan (1997)
                  Volunteered for inner-city project to assist poor readers to improve their
                  reading scores before going back to school in the fall. Results: 87 percent
                  of students who attended the class improved their reading 1 to 2 grade
                  levels as measured by national tests.

Dona Frank   Voice: (656) 879-4326
3278 Main Street   Office: (656) 897-6754
Dayton, Montana 00000   e-mail: BunnyFrank@000.edu

POSITION: <u>Elementary School Reading Specialist</u>. Jackson County School
                   District, #4. Moraine City, Michigan (1997–present)

SKILLS: (Wide variety of responsibilities within the district.)

Primary	Elementary	Administration
Vocabulary Drills	Reading Labs	Interdistrict Plans
Comprehension	Tests and Measures	Primary-Level View
Teacher Training	Comprehension	Gr. 4, 5, and 6 Designs

                   Other skills such as classroom management, teacher-student liai-
                   son, parent-teacher conferences, and individual student counseling
                   occur at various times and situations within each month.

PROFESSIONAL   Designed and implemented a new system for testing intermediate
ACCOMPLISHMENTS: reading comprehension twice a year, resulting in better student per-
                   formance on national tests.

                   Developed three grade levels within each primary division for more
                   accurate measure of vocabulary skills, resulting in better compre-
                   hension and extended vocabulary among the three grade levels.

                   Designed a comprehensive teacher-training program for all teachers
                   of primary students, resulting in early diagnosis of reading difficul-
                   ties among students in grades 1, 2, and 3.

EDUCATION: **M.A. (Elementary Reading Education)** University of Michigan. Ann
                   Arbor, Michigan
                   Current topics under study include psychology of reading, child
                   physical and mental development, contemporary learning theories,
                   and children's literature.

                   B.S. (Elementary Education) University of Southern Michigan.
                   Jackson, Michigan, *cum laude*

Appendix I

CAREER PLANNER

Career Planner is designed to assist you in keeping track of all the information you need to conduct a professional job search. This includes a *Personal Information* file for your land address, e-mail addresses and phone and FAX numbers, plus a record of your educational accomplishments and experience of work, with supervisor's names, company addresses, phone and fax numbers, etc.

Also included is a file titled *Letters,* where you can keep templates for cover letters or pitch letters used for various position types. Several are available: target, broadcast, network, market mini résumé, acceptance, and withdrawal, as well as memorandum of record.

The *Career Planner* contains a file where you can store information related to interviews, leads to companies, records of meetings, and any potential need for follow-up or criticism of what happened with each company.

In addition, a *Calendar* has been added so that you can actually see the dates and times of appointments for the month.

Your instructor's materials contain details on how to use each section of the *Career Planner.* Access to this disk will be made available to those who are using the textbook at the request of their instructor. Each school will have its own directives and processes for making the disk available to students. If you are using this text on your own, consider requesting the disk and accompanying materials from Prentice Hall.

GLOSSARY

CAREER

benefits package: Combination of benefits that have a monetary value and are 25 to 30 percent of one's total compensation. These may include bonuses, box seats, car or travel allowance, company car, credit cards, education cap and tuition reimbursement, expense accounts, identified leave, holidays, insurance, outplacement, pensions, professional control, stock options, trailing-spouse accommodations, and other items negotiated by the job candidate and the company negotiator.

candidate: Individual implementing a career search after graduation from college.

career centers: Identified separate places in libraries where career searchers can research data.

career focus: Larger career goal than that specified as career objective on the résumé.

career objective: Clearly focused goal statement of place, skill, and reason to hire that introduces the résumé.

career search: The marketing method whereby a graduate designs and implements the best and most professional way to uncover the best job opportunity available at the time.

compensation: Combination of salary plus benefits in exchange for services and skills provided for the employer.

consultants: Individuals who have specific skills that are in demand and are willing to move from company to company performing their skills.

Curriculum Vitae: Complete list of one's accomplishments, publications, awards, and prior employment; still used in Europe and in Japan, also for academic positions.

dream job: That position the candidate feels most completely matches his or her career objective.

earnings power: How much compensation one is able to negotiate given the market and the person's history of earning.

entrepreneur: A risk taker who believes in the ideas or projects generated and who is willing to strike out individually if necessary to work in the desired field.

four Ps: Marketing mix that is deemed successful in selling a new product or service; its elements include price, place, product, and promotion.

Game Theory: Theory developed by John vonNeumann in a book of the same name to enable people to make valid decisions among variables that are not equal but can be based within mathematical equations.

graduate placement: Offices on campuses whose role is a combination of job interview preparation, support record keeping, and counsel to graduates of the school.

hidden market: Unlisted but existing positions; created positions make this list.

house-hunting expenses: To be negotiated by the job applicant; may include other adult decision maker and the applicant's separate or extended trip to explore the housing market. This includes travel, lodging, and food, but it must be negotiated.

HRM: Human resources management. Usually responsible for interviewing activity.

indigenous benefits: Those benefits that come because of an individual's position in the company or are made available to all employees because the products or services are natural to the company.

InfoTrac: CD-ROM package available to libraries that includes "Business Profiles" and "Magazine Files" that can be made available to searchers by topic, name, geographic area, field, or career. This information can then be printed for the searcher.

interviews: Face-to-face communication, conversational style, to determine information. Can be conducted for evaluation, information, job, negotiation, and style determination of a company and of a candidate. Interviews may also be conducted by electronic means today.

intrepreneur: Individual who functions as an entrepreneur but is within a company, often the head of a specific division in which the person's expertise is in demand.

job: Industrial age icon that describes work for hire in the industrial age.

job search: Another name for career search. Can be conducted using traditional tools, contemporary networking methods, and/or electronic means available to a searcher. In-house searching is also possible for those who want to improve their positions within the company currently employing them.

keyword stripe: Line of 45 to 60 characters that highlights one's skills, degrees, and employment and is placed at the top of the résumé before the personal identification data.

knowledge workers: Individuals whose heads are valued more than their hands.

marketplace: Work environments of chosen careers.

memorandum of record: Written statement of job acceptance that includes listing of negotiated items. Candidate also asks for verification of understanding by a certain date.

mini résumé: Résumé designed as a business letter aimed at top executives; used only at the end of a campaign if the dream job is still not forthcoming.

moving expenses: Expenses to be remunerated to the candidate on submission of vouchers or some other system. These include movers' fees, stays in motels, and lodging while household goods are transported (covers candidate and all dependents). Must be negotiated; cannot be assumed.

naysayer: Individual who always sees the dark side of things.

negotiate: Process of give and take that results in a candidate and a company agreeing on terms of employment.

outplacement: Negotiated approach to placing a valued employee elsewhere because of company policy that forces the employee out of a job through no fault of that employee.

part-time worker: Individual whose services and skills are available for hire, usually through a temporary-placement agency and on a short-term basis.

partnership: Private business group of similar or various backgrounds who agree to support, run, and oversee a chosen business resulting in shared profits at the end of successful years for these partners.

placement: The practice of arranging for an employee to be hired for a specific responsibility.

power lunch: 1990s name for business lunch among colleagues or professionals.

prospects: List of individuals to be seen as part of a search campaign or sales tool.

résumé: Tool to announce a candidate's readiness, preparation, and interest in a career field. Résumé may appear in a variety of formats, but the information remains the same in all.

salary: First step in a negotiations process to assign monetary value to one's compensation with respect to candidate's accumulated skills and company needs identification.

skill: Keyword in current search campaigns. Companies are looking for and will pay for skilled people. High priority of information identified on a résumé.

sole proprietorship: Individual- or family-owned business.

succession charts: Method for identifying people, process, and method for promotion within a company structure.

technician: New definition to accommodate the knowledge worker who defines skills acquired in technical terms, thus translating for the résumé reader what is significant about how individuals use their knowledge and degree.

temporary worker: Another name for part-time worker.

trailing spouse: Current term to identify individual for whom the new employee is negotiating terms because these individuals are usually in professional positions themselves, which they have to give up for the potential employee to move and accept a position.

translator: Job searcher must be able to translate capabilities for the reader of the résumé, the interviewer for the job, and the negotiator for compensation.

wage earner: Individual who gets paid for the practice and use of his or her skills and knowledge.

10K report: Similar to an annual report but in greater depth; prepared for SEC when a company petitions to change its position on the stock exchanges.

401K pension plans: Pension options available for most employees in good companies.

90-day review: Opportunity to assess one's performance and receive a raise within the first year.

TECHNICAL

ADF: Automatic document feeder. Feeds documents into fax machines without operator assistance.

America Online: One of many commercial services that provide access to the Internet.

analogue transmission: Traditional telephone technology in which sound waves or other information is converted to electronic impulses of varying lengths.

applets: Mini programs that can be downloaded quickly and used by any computer equipped with a Java-capable browser. Applets carry their own software players.

ASCII: American standard code for information interchange. Seven-bit coding system represents data for processing and communications. Text characters are faxed over phone lines.

bps: Bits per second. The number of data bits sent per second between two modems; measures the rate at which the information is handled, manipulated, or transferred.

bit: One binary digit, either 0 or 1.

bus: The group of conductors that interconnect individual circuitry in a computer.

byte: Eight related bits of data; an 8-bit binary number.

cable modem: Connects computer to high-speed coaxial line carrying a cable TV signal into the home. Can receive data at speeds of up to 10 million bits per second (bps), about 700 times faster than the 14,000-bps modems many use today.

cache: High-speed processor memory that buffers commonly used instructions or data.

CD-ROM: Flat laser disk used to store information at greater density than floppy disks.

computer age: From ca. 1975 to today.

CPU: Central processing unit. The part of the computer that controls the hardware during operations.

coaxial cable: Transmission line with a central core that conducts electricity. Coaxial cable can transmit more information than a pair of twisted copper wires, which are commonly used for telephone communication.

cyberspace: Where Web sites go to be organized and made available to Internet users.

digital age: The time when analogue technology has been replaced by digital technology.

digital transmission: Converts sound waves and other information into binary computer code, which is a series of zeros and ones. The binary code is converted back when it reaches its destination.

DIO: Digital input/output.

disk: A thin, flat plate inserted into a plastic cover, size 5 1/4 or 3 1/2 inches. A data disk is used to store information/data from computer operations. A demonstration disk is used to demonstrate a product or service. Computer information systems scientists design the programs for software use: word processing, spreadsheet, games, graphics, design, and so on.

DRAM: Dynamic random access memory. Volatile storage that may not be interrupted; if it is, information will be lost.

dumb terminal: A computing unit with a keyboard and screen but no internal memory; it functions as an input–display unit only.

e-mail: Electronic mail. Transfers text messages, memos, and reports over a network.

electronic media: Means of dispersing information and data by electrons over fiber-optic cables.

emoticon: Punctuation symbols typed sideways to communicate messages through e-mail :) : (

fourth-generation language: Programming language not so heavily reliant on code as its predecessors.

Genie: Search engine for the Internet through Netscape.

gigabyte: 1 billion bytes, or 1,000 megabytes.

gopher: Internet browsing server in which information is arranged by menus.

hardware: All the technical tools that are used in computer operations other than the software programs and databases: computer, printer, peripherals, mouse, and so forth.

home page: Display on the WWW that usually identifies and describes the page owner and contains links to other pages.

HTML: Hypertext markup language. Common language of Web documents.

http: Hypertext transfer protocol. Allows for instant, seamless transfer of information across the Web.

hypertext: Text and graphics in Web documents can be linked to text and graphics in other Web documents; they are accessed with a simple mouse click.

Internet: World's largest network, consisting of 10,500 individual networks supporting nearly 2 million computers, linking governments, universities, and commercial institutions.

ISDN: Integrated Services Digital Network. Digital network that supports high-speed transfer of fax, data, voice, and video over standard copper telephone wire at speeds of up to 128,000 bps in the digital format computers can process.

JAVA: Programming language from Sun Microsystems allowing animations, sounds, and instant updates of information.

Jughead: Tool to search specific Web site.

LAN: Local area network. Telecommunication links and networks within a local area.

LED: Light-emitting diode. An array of pixel-size lights within a stationary printhead.

Lycos: A search engine that helps you locate resources by keywords.

mainframe computer: Manages large amounts of data and complex computing tasks. Also describes memory storage and the computing part of a large computer system.

MB: megabyte. Equals 1 million bytes.

microcomputer: PC based on a single-chip processor.

microfiche: Microfilm that contains rows of pages in reduced form.

Microsoft Office: Set of software packages, Access, Excel, Mail, PowerPoint, Project, and Word, for use separately or in combination for word processing, spreadsheets, graphics, e-mail, calendars, and so forth.

minicomputer: Medium-size computer running a multitasking operating system capable of managing 100 users simultaneously.

modem: *Mo*dulate/*Dem*odulate. The sending modem converts digital data to analogue form; receiving modem converts analogue signal back to digital.

Monster Board: Popular graphical Web browser and database for job hunters; emphasis is east of the Mississippi.

Mosaic: Very popular graphical Web browser and database for job hunters; emphasis is west of the Mississippi.

multimedia: Hardware and software capable of delivering not only text but also digitized voice, image, and video presentations of information.

multitasking: Several processors can be run simultaneously.

Net: Shortened form of *Internet.*

netiquette: Proper etiquette when communicating over the Internet.

Netscape: Network browser currently replacing Mosaic.

network: Connected cables through which a variety of information, data, and messages can flow within and among organizations, regions, neighborhoods, satellites, TVs, and so forth.

newsgroup: A discussion group on a specific topic, maintained on a computer network or a bulletin board.

Newsnet: Sophisticated electronic news clipping service. Provides latest information daily. Great preparation for interviews for which you need recent company information.

object-oriented database: Database organized around an object model rather than the conventional models.

object-oriented technology: Computer programming that builds software applications through repeated use of self-contained objects—bits of data that are surrounded with the program information needed to gain access to the data. Objects can perform certain computer functions when they receive messages to do that function.

OCR: Optical character recognition. A scanning device to convert paper documents to electronic alphanumeric characters that can be stored in a computer.

PowerPoint: A graphics production software within Microsoft Office using a Windows environment.

protocol: Exact sequence of bits, characters, and control codes used to transfer data between computers and peripherals through a communications channel.

résumé: Electronic résumés include all résumés made and communicated by means of electronic disks, CD-ROMs, in ASCII text, with multimedia, videotapes, slide presentations, and over the WWW with a Web home page. They may or may not be interactive. All require a computer to decipher. Some are stand-alone disks with directions about how to access the data; others require a certain standard of operating system or software packages to access the data.

software: Disks that are individually or commercially programmed for business operations using computers or personal computer operations such as games.

stand-alone program: A compiled program that runs with the operating system but without any other software programs or environments.

Telnet: Program that allows you to move all over the world and select files electronically from computers nearby or far away.

Turbo C, C++: Object-oriented programming software package.

URL: Uniform resource locator. File name of any object that can be addressed on the Web, point on an HTML page, graphic in a directory, or even an executable script.

Usenet: A large group of networks and computers that organizes messages by newsgroup; a branch of the Internet.

user-friendly: Term used to indicate that a software package will be easy to use for the nontechnical person who needs what the program provides.

Veronica: A frequently updated index system intended to make gopher even easier to use.

videotape: A videotaped record of information, data, slides, multimedia, and so on.

visibility: Candidates for jobs can make themselves visible to employers twenty-four hours a day by using the technology currently available.

Visual Basic: A fourth-generation database programming language.

voice telephone: E-mail or other mechanisms for sending and receiving messages.

WAN: Wide area network. Long-distance telecommunication links and networks that connect local area networks and end stations regionally, nationally, or internationally.

Web: Text, graphics, video, and sound used separately or in combination to produce a site or to develop a home page.

Windows: Operating system from Microsoft.

word processing: Using computers and software programs to type, arrange, correct, and improve typed copy of business or personal information and store on a floppy disk.

WWW: World Wide Web. A popular and rapidly growing new medium of human communication that encompasses text, graphics, video, and sound and is available instantly anywhere in the world.

Yahoo: Collection of Web- and Internet-based information categorized in a subject tree.

INDEXES

NAME INDEX

RESEARCH INDEX

SUBJECT INDEX